Magnificent Obsession:

Following Hard After God

By Eric Watt

www.ericwatt.com
January 2014

Magnificent Obsession: Following Hard After God
By Eric Watt

Printed in the United States of America

ISBN-13: 978-1495216411

The world has yet to see what God can do with and for and through and in and by the man who is fully and wholly consecrated to Him.

I will try my utmost to be that man.

D.L. Moody

FORWARD

For nearly a quarter of a century I have made it my life's passion to follow whole-hardheartedly and passionately after God. The single pursuit to follow Jesus and share His gift of love and forgiveness with others who have never heard the Good News has taken me to the high deserts of China, through the jungles of SE Asia, across the steppes of Central Asia, down the Hindu Kush of the Indian Subcontinent and throughout the Middle East. At each stop I have asked the Lord for new friendships, new experiences and a fresh perspective of His plans for the world. I have seen my share of hardship and pain along the way, but they could never compare to the blessings I have received.

At the beginning of my journey I was filled with knowledge, strategy, ambition and know-how...or so I thought. Over the years I have come to learn that the best "nuggets" I have passed along to others did not come from my lectures, teaching or preaching, but rather from sharing my heart for prayer and the simple truths I learned from God's Word.

During the course of my own journey I have "stumbled" across amazing saints serving our infinitely gracious and loving God. They have inspired me as we worked together on small unknown projects and large endeavors that were public and fairly high profile. My greatest treasure, however, has not been in what we accomplished, but in the life we shared as we followed hard after God.

One day I hope be able to share their stories, but for the sake of their own security and safety that day will have to wait. In the meanwhile, I have decided to compile some of the life lessons we have shared in this daily prayer journal – “Magnificent Obsession: Following Hard After God.”

Eric Watt

Day 1

You are Incredible, God!

A Truth to Live – God's destiny for me requires my complete devotion to Him.

Scripture – *"Love the Lord your God with all your heart and with all your soul and with all your mind and with all your strength...Love your neighbor as yourself."* Mark 12:30-31

Prayer – God, You are incredible! To think that before my day began You had already carefully designed a way for me to find meaning and purpose in my life. I don't even have to search to find the bounty of Your love for me. You made the world, the sun, the moon, the stars and everything good on this earth.

It is to You that I devote my best. I give You the emotions and passions of my heart. You have the freedom to shape my personality and character, to create in my mind a reflection of Your wisdom. Your plan for me is so great; Your eternal destiny beyond description, my only response is to honor You with who I am.

Take total control of me today. I commit to You the care of my whole being...every part of me is Yours. Use me to bring peace to Your world. In Jesus' name, Amen.

Day 2

Today I Choose to Join Your Mission

A Truth to Live – My purpose in life is found in living out His purposes.

Scripture – *"The reason the Son of God appeared was to destroy the Devil's work."* I John 3:8

Prayer – God, today I ask for Your wisdom to increase in my life. There are so many tasks and responsibilities that pull on me every day. In fact, most of the time, my life seems too busy to add just one more thing. Sometimes I lose the priority focus that made Jesus' life so fruitful and satisfying.

Would You take me beyond what I think is important and place in me the determination to live like Jesus? Through the power of Your love I want to destroy the work of evil and make a difference in my world. To my family, my friends and colleagues I want to see the crippling impact of evil be destroyed by the simple, but powerful, demonstration of Your never ending and gentle love. It made all the difference in my life, now I want to see Your love change those I know are trapped by the evils of this world. In Jesus' name, Amen.

Day 3

You Have Authority Over This World

A Truth to Live – God has transferred His eternal authority to those who follow Him. From now on I will live in the eternal destiny which God has laid out for me. I will walk in His spiritual authority and share the simple, but powerful Good News with my world. I know this means much more than reciting words – I must also be His hands and feet.

Scripture – *"All authority in heaven and on earth has been given to me. Therefore go and make disciples of all nations, baptizing them in the name of the Father and of the Son and of the Holy Spirit, and teaching them to obey everything I have commanded you. And surely I am with you always, to the very end of the age."* Matthew 28:18-20

Prayer – Help me, Lord, and grant me the strength to obey You and teach others to do the same. Even when I feel hesitant or alone in doing Your will, I will remember that Your very presence is with me when I walk according to Your Word.

Thank You, God. You are empowering me today to live beyond myself. You want me to be involved in the BIG plan of the ages – taking Your Good News to every person in every community on earth. Show me today how to take the first steps in Your grand purposes! In Jesus' name, Amen.

Day 4

You Made Us to Love

A Truth to Live – God is love and loving God means loving others. From the beginning of time God's original design was for me to love others.

I John 4:7 says, *"Let us love one another, for love comes from God. Everyone who loves has been born of God and knows God."* This is how I can know that the power of the Gospel rules in me – if I have love for all people regardless of their race, religion, gender, or behavior. You loved me, and I am to love others.

Scripture – *"Love the Lord your God with all your heart and with all your soul and with all your mind. This is the first commandment. And second is like it: Love your neighbor as yourself."* Matthew 22:37-39

Prayer – Today I commit to love You with every part of my being. I will use all my energy to grow in my relationship with You – learning and listening for Your voice throughout my day.

And, just as I will use my heart, soul and mind to love You, I will also use my all to love others. I will begin today looking at my family, my colleagues, my schoolmates, my neighbors, my friends and Your world through the eyes of love. Lord, I ask that You pour Your love out on me today so that I can give it freely to others. In Jesus' name, Amen.

Day 5

It's Time to Make a Difference

A Truth to Live – God wants to give His supernatural power to me so that I can be a witness for Him in my world.

The greatest treasure in my life is that the God of the universe chooses to work through me! Even though I am undeserving and not qualified, His promises are still true. I can count on His power working through me today. In fact, Jeremiah 1:12 says that He is "watching to see that [His] Word is fulfilled."

Scripture: *"But you will receive power when the Holy Spirit comes on you; and you will be my witnesses in Jerusalem, and in all Judea and Samaria, and to the ends of the earth."* Acts 1:8

Prayer – Heavenly Father, today I choose to spend time in Your presence, waiting for the power of Your Holy Spirit to guide and empower my day. I will listen to Your voice and follow the path that You lay down for me. You have promised that I would play a role in seeing the Good News spread from me to those near me – to family and friends, to my community and to the whole world. Thank You for allowing me to participate in Your master plan for redemption. I am ready to be used to see my world transformed. In Jesus' name, Amen.

Day 6

Living on Purpose

A Truth to Live – God has given me a divine purpose for my life!

Today is a day of divine destiny for my life. Because God promises to "direct my steps" (Proverbs 16:9) when I honor Him with my life, I can count on God's interaction and intervention at every turn.

Scripture – *"For when David had served God's purpose in his own generation, he fell asleep..."* Acts 13:32

Prayer – Lord, I am asking You to visit me today and to instruct me in the "way that I should go" (Psalm 32:8). Reveal to me Your divine destiny so that I can fulfill Your purposes in my life. This means more to me than the compliments of others or the momentary pleasure of a task accomplished. I live for You and will walk according to Your purpose. In Jesus' name, Amen.

Day 7

Commissioned to the World

A Truth to Live – God's purpose for me is to deliver His message in my world.

Scripture – *"As you sent me into the world, I have sent them into the world."* John 17:18

Prayer – You are my example, God. How awesome You are to send me a Savior, Friend and Guide. There are times that the distractions in my life make it very hard to actually know what I am about and where I should be going. It's in these times that I am so grateful that You sent Jesus into my life and commissioned me in the power of Your Spirit to live a life modeled after Jesus.

I admit that on my own this is impossible, but also acknowledge that with You "nothing is impossible." (Luke 1:37) So today, I stand on the reality that You make the impossible possible. You have placed me in Your Body and You promise to use me - with all my shortcomings - to deliver the Good News to Your world. In Jesus' name, Amen.

Day 8

He is in Charge of My Destiny

A Truth to Live – I can rest assured that the God who created me is able to fulfill His promises in me.

Scripture – *"The Lord works out everything for His purposes."* Proverbs 16:4

Prayer – God, You are all powerful. As I begin my day I can take comfort in the reality that You are working out the details of my life for good. From the beginning of time You have had my best interests in mind. Rather than trying to work harder to "get things right" today I begin with the first step toward my own destiny – I surrender to the plans that You have for me.

Lord, I put my life in Your hands. Mold me today into a useful vessel in Your Kingdom. Set in motion Your destiny in my life – to bring Your peace to my world. I look forward with great expectation to see Your hand at work in me and through me. In Jesus' name, Amen.

Day 9

He Has Good for Me to Do

A Truth to Live – God has already planned out His destiny for my life.

God is in control. The circumstances around me do not define me because God himself is in control. He is the one who has crafted my very existence, designed my personality, given expression to my interests and passions. He has taken interest in me!

Scripture – *"For we are God's workmanship, created in Christ Jesus to good works, which God prepared in advance for us to do."* Ephesians 2:10

Prayer – How grateful I am to You, God. You not only set the universe in motion but You also have taken care to insure that my life finds meaning in something greater than myself. You have planned out my days and, when I listen to You, I find hope in learning that You have prepared my life's path with good things to do.

Today I choose Your way, Your works, and Your presence. I will not yield to the cravings of my own flesh, nor the demands of my circumstances. I will seek You and Your Kingdom and then watch You go to work in me and through me! In Jesus' name, Amen.

Day 10

My Life Is Made With Purpose

A Truth to Live – I have been given a purpose to accomplish in life.

I was made for one thing. My gifts, abilities, passion, experience and personality have been uniquely combined for one single reason. It is THE task of my life to testify to those around me of the Good News of God's grace.

Scripture – *"...I consider my life worth nothing to me, if only I may finish the race and complete the task the Lord Jesus has given me – the task of testifying to the gospel of God's grace."* Acts 20:24

Prayer – Lord, I need You to remind me of my destiny. There are so many distractions surrounding me each and every day that I can easily forget what really counts. You are the only thing worth living for. You have made such a difference in my life, and I want to testify to others of Your greatness. I ask You to create opportunities in my conversations today, and grant me the privilege to share Your Good News with others. In Jesus' name, Amen.

Day 11

God Has Given Me Work to Do

A Truth to Live – I bring glory to God when I fulfill His mission in my life.

Scripture – *"I have brought you glory on earth by completing the work you gave me to do."* John 17:4

Prayer – Jesus, You are my example, and I want to follow in Your steps. You brought glory to Your Heavenly Father by completing Your work here on earth, and I choose today to do the same. The work that You have given for me to do will become my highest priority.

I will make wise choices today to honor You with my behavior, my conduct, my conversation with others and the integrity of my own thoughts. I know that You have divinely placed me at home, school or work to make an impact for You, and I will share Your story in my life with those around me.

Beginning today, knowing that my life gives You glory is the only satisfaction that I need. I ask, Lord, that You give me strength to walk consistently and have ears to hear clearly so that I can bring You glory. In Jesus' name, Amen.

Day 12

My Life As An Adventure

A Truth to Live – Following Jesus is the adventure of a lifetime! God has my absolute best in mind.

Sometimes it seems that God's ways are more difficult or personally challenging. But, I know from experience that going my own way does not often end in good. In fact, left to my own directions, my path usually comes to a dead end.

Scripture – *"If anyone would come after me, he must deny himself and take up his cross daily and follow me."* Luke 9:23

Prayer – Father, today, I will start a new path, chart a new course. I will forego my own impulses and ideas, choosing instead to follow the Jesus way. It is not the way of self-promotion or self-satisfaction, but it is the way of fulfillment. Following You, Jesus, requires thoughtful discipline and a consistent choosing of the Kingdom way. Lord, empower me today to carry Your cross and inspire me to follow Your better way. In Jesus' name, Amen.

Day 13

God's Anointing is For Me

A Truth to Live – God's direction for my life involves blessing others.

Scripture – *The Spirit of the Sovereign Lord is on me, because the Lord has anointed me to preach the good news to the poor, He has sent me to bind up the brokenhearted, to proclaim freedom for the captives and release from darkness for the prisoners."* Isaiah 61:1

Prayer – God, You have chosen the right direction for my life. When the clutter and busyness of my life crowd Your purpose for me, help me to remember that my real fulfillment comes when I give back to others. In fact, when I concentrate on my own needs, I am left with my own feeble wisdom to try to solve the problem. But when I bring the Good News to those in need, Your anointing flows through my life – bringing healing to me and to so many others around me.

Help me to remember that just as You gave Your life for me, I should spend my life serving others. Your blessing flows in my life when I help meet the needs of the poor, encourage the brokenhearted, help those bound in emotional pain, and care for those in prison. Place my life today, Lord, with others who are in need. Give me the chance to pour out so that I can be a vessel filled with Your eternal never ending goodness. In Jesus' name, Amen.

Day 14

God Grants Eternal Blessing

A Truth to Live – God grants mercy to those who love Him and judgment to those who oppose Him.

Scripture – *"The Spirit of the Sovereign Lord is on me…to proclaim the year of the Lord's favor and the day of vengeance of our God."* Isaiah 61:1-2

Prayer – Today, Lord I ask for strength to be about Your business. You have asked me to proclaim to others Your great favor and forgiveness. You desire for every person to experience bountiful blessing when they respond to You in love and submission. I cannot imagine my life without Your direction and leadership. I gladly turn over my fears of what others might think of me, trading them in for Your anointing and provision.

Grant me wisdom in my interaction with others, that I might be able to share Your nature and character with them. You desire to show mercy and love to all those who call upon You to be saved. If people resist You, then they are choosing a Day of Judgment and vengeance. I trust You to right all wrongs and to bring every person to an opportunity of forgiveness and blessing. You are filled with love, mercy and wisdom. I trust You and know that Your heart is for them. I pray today that my friends and family, plus those in this world would find favor in Your eyes. In Jesus' name, Amen.

Day 15

God Uses His Servants to Bless Those in Need

A Truth to Live – God's blessings flow through those who meet the needs of others.

Scripture – *"The Spirit of the Sovereign Lord is on me…to comfort all who mourn and provide for those who grieve in Zion – to bestow on them a crown of beauty instead of ashes, the oil of gladness instead of mourning, and a garment of praise instead of a spirit of despair."* Isaiah 61:1-3

Prayer – God, You have chosen me to make an impact in my world. It is no longer enough to cry out to You for my own needs. You desire that I meet the real and practical needs of those who are wounded, those who mourn and those whose life is torn apart by despair. With access to Your Word and the authority of the Spirit of Jesus residing in me I can do it! I can do all things through You.

I am prepared today and ask for Your grace to begin bringing hope to those who are wounded by the hardships of life. Grant to me supernatural wisdom and understanding to pass along Your goodness to others. In Jesus' name, Amen.

Day 16

God Desires to Work Through Me

A Truth to Live – God can do the impossible through me.

Scripture – *"I am the Lord, the God of all mankind. Is anything too hard for me?"* Jeremiah 32:27

Prayer – Sometimes, Lord, I am faced with difficulties that seem too hard for me. The impact of these trials clouds my thinking and distorts my understanding. This is when I cry out to You and ask for Your Word to begin to work in my life.

I admit that most of my life, even my walk with You has been about me and not about You or Your world. Do the impossible in my life and take me down a new path that focuses on blessing others first. I know that the impossible will start in my life when I begin passing along Your goodness to others. This will take a miracle for me, but I entrust my future to Your hands; they are more than capable. In Jesus' name, Amen.

Day 17

God's Power Can Be at Work in Me

A Truth to Live – God's Spiritual power is available to those who follow Him.

Scripture – *"You shall receive power when the Holy Spirit comes on you; and you will be my witnesses in Jerusalem, and in all Judea and Samaria, and to the ends of the earth."* Acts 1:8

Prayer – God, Your promises are true, always true. They are true when You promise that Your own Spirit will be poured out on all of Your followers. I admit that many days I start off in my own strength and intentions. I do not wait for Your Spirit's instructions and power.

Beginning today, things will be different. I will listen to Your Holy Spirit and obey Your words. I expect Your miracle working power to begin to work through me. I commit to join with others to make a difference in my world and even to those in other nations. I expect Your power to move through me! In Jesus' name, Amen.

Day 18

Everyone Can Know

A Truth to Live – There is one way for the whole world to know Him.

Scripture – *"By this all men will know that you are my disciples, if you love one another."* John 13:35

Prayer – Your greatest command is to love. I know that above all else I should love You, and I should love others. Easy words to say, but honestly actually loving others is not the easiest to live. For me, my own desires seem to easily drown out the demonstration of my love for others – especially when it is an inconvenience to my own plans.

But You have a different plan for me. It is not a plan that requires heroic effort in my part or super-human talent. You are asking me today to love others with my words and actions. For me the simplest way to accomplish this mission is to stay focused on the unequalled love You have shown me.

Lord, today I yield to Your love, and I ask You to grant me the privilege of passing it on to others. In Jesus' name, Amen.

Encourage One Another!

A Truth to Live – The world is waiting to see us demonstrate His love.

Scripture – *"Let us consider how we may spur one another on toward love and good deeds."* Hebrews 10:24

Prayer – Thank You, God for surrounding me in a community of believers. Though I sometimes act without their input and guidance, You have my best interest in mind by providing me meaningful relationships to challenge and grow me as a person.

Today, I choose to connect with those You have placed in my life. I will encourage them to stretch beyond their patterns of comfort and love others by what they do and say. At the same time I ask You to make me teachable, so that I can learn from others and see Your goodness poured out in my life through them. As we commit to encourage one another, surely those around us will see You shining brightly in our world. In Jesus' name, Amen.

Day 20

God Designed Me to Grow

A Truth to Live – We learn best by doing life together.

Scripture -- *"They devoted themselves to the apostles' teaching and to the fellowship, to the breaking of bread and to prayer."* Acts 2:42

Prayer – I choose to follow Your truth today, God. Even though there are so many "things" that I could give my attention to, I have decided that from now on, I am going to do it Your way. Not only will I place You first in my life, but I will also connect myself with those You have placed in my life. You created me to share my life with and to learn from those who have walked farther down life's journey.

Lord, today I position myself as a learner, ready to soak in Your truth and to grow. I commit to follow through with what I learn and begin to put it into practice. In order for me to stay consistent I choose to make myself accountable to others who are growing in the same direction. Together we can experience the best that You have for us. In Jesus' name, Amen.

Day 21

We Can Do More Together

A Truth to Live – God blesses those who work together.

Scripture – "*All the believers were one in heart and mind.*" Acts 4:32

Prayer – Lord, today I desire to experience Your divine power in my life just like the believers did in the 1st century church. They had a special relationship with one another – sharing their possessions with one another and living out their days with the same heart, the same passions, and the same focus.

I ask today that You would grant me the privilege of locking arms with other believers to better accomplish the tasks You have put in front of me. I will no longer go it alone, but will instead seek to discover Your wisdom, understanding and direction at work in the lives of those You have brought in my path. Together we can be stronger, than we could ever be alone. In Jesus' name, Amen.

Day 22

God is Commissioning Me

A Truth to Live – When I seek God, I can expect His direction.

Scripture – "*Set apart for me Barnabas and Saul for the work to which I have called them.*" Acts 13:2

Prayer – Lord, Your destiny for my life is not a haphazard thought on Your part. You have already declared that before ideas spring into being, You are there to shape my mind and heart to be ready for Your abundant blessing. I am eager to belong to a spiritual community where, through prayer and worship, we can receive Your revelation. Just as You sent out Barnabas and Saul for a specific work, so You desire to do the same in my life.

I am ready to be connected with Your spiritual family and commissioned into Your world. I will LISTEN and OBEY Your promptings today, expecting great and mighty things from you. In Jesus' name, Amen.

Day 23

God Grants the Power to Obey and to Go

A Truth to Live – He has the power to shape my world.

Scripture – "*You will receive power when the Holy Spirit comes on you; and you will be my witness in Jerusalem, and in all Judea and Samaria and to the ends of the earth.*" Acts 1:8

Prayer – God, just as the disciples waited to receive power from You, I choose to wait for the presence of Your Holy Spirit to saturate my life. I know that through my own strength the obstacles before me cannot be moved. But with You all things are possible!

Baptize me anew today in Your purity and power. I shake off the hindrances that keep me from going 100% for You. Fill me with supernatural power and move through me with Your spiritual gifts. I will be Your witness today, wherever You choose and whenever You direct. I know that You have a plan for me to do "normal things" that will change the world. I choose to place my expectations on You and You alone. I make myself available to be used by You today. In Jesus' name, Amen.

Day 24

Knit Together for Life

A Truth to Live – God has given me people to learn from and share with.

Scripture – *"And the things you have heard me say in the presence of many witnesses entrust to reliable men who will also be qualified to teach others."*
2 Timothy 2:2

Prayer – God, You are all-wise and all-knowing. I depend on You every day for wisdom and guidance, both for the big plans and the everyday decisions. Even though You threw the stars into their place and set even the most finite detail of our world in motion – today I am amazed at how You take time for me.

I will listen to those You place around me. Whether a colleague or a family member, I trust You to speak through them. I will watch and learn from the leaders You have given me. And, I will be an example to those I influence. In this way Your influence can spread from one generation to another, till the whole earth knows You! In Jesus' name, Amen.

Day 25

Ordained for a Purpose

A Truth to Live – God has ordained me to share the Good News.

Scripture – *"Believe in the Lord Jesus, and you will be saved – you and your household."* Acts 16:31

Prayer – I have confidence in my day, Lord, because the world You created is still in Your care. From the beginning of time You chose to place me in relationship with people who need Your love. I commit today to allow my own inhibitions to give way to the enormous compassion You have for my friends and family.

Today, I choose to be a conduit for You. You have empowered me to share the simple but powerful truth and I will be faithful to You. I expect conversations to "go there" and to be able to answer the questions I am asked. I will gently guide my friends and family to You and watch You do amazing things through me. In Jesus' name, Amen.

Day 26

Guided by the Holy Spirit

A Truth to Live – God is active in my everyday life.

Scripture – *"During the night Paul had a vision of a man…begging him to 'come over to Macedonia and help us.' So Paul…got ready at once to…preach the Gospel to them."* Acts 16:9-10

Prayer – God, You desire to make Your will known to me. Whether I am going about my daily routine or sleeping, I will look today for Your supernatural direction. I am confident that You are orchestrating my circumstances so that those near to me will be open and receptive to Your encouraging Word and the transforming story You are working in me.

Today, Lord, is the day You have created. I look forward to listening and acting on Your Word so that I might bring the revelation of who You are to others. In Jesus' name, Amen.

Day 27

God Sends Me Out to Fulfill My Destiny

A Truth to Live – God empowers His children to meet every challenge.

Scripture – *"The two of them, sent on their way by the Holy Spirit."* Acts 13:4

Prayer – God, You are the only One who satisfies. Your Spirit empowers me every day and provides me the daily direction I need. I am so grateful that as I face my struggles You bring clarity and purpose. Rather than try to find my own way today, I choose to allow You to direct my path, order my steps and make clear the words I am to share with others.

My destiny will be fulfilled when I cling to Your ways and willingly follow the gentle whisperings of Your Spirit. Speak to me today, Lord and I will obey Your Word. In Jesus' name, Amen.

Day 28

God's Spirit Assures My Destiny

A Truth to Live – Your Spirit compels me to fulfill my destiny.

Scripture – *"Compelled by the Spirit, I am going to Jerusalem."* Acts 20:22

Prayer – I choose to be dependent on You today. You can see ahead of me and know the path I should walk. Rather than attempt to discover my steps, I will await Your direction, knowing that Your destiny for me is wrapped up in Your heart for the world.

Use me, Lord, beyond my own plans and dreams. Help me to focus on changing Your world, not just the familiar. You deserve to receive glory from the whole earth. I commit to use the gifts and skills You have given me to make a difference for You. In Jesus' name, Amen.

Day 29

God's Power is for a Purpose

A Truth to Live – God empowers me to all nations.

Scripture – "*You shall receive power when the Holy Spirit comes on you; and you will be my witnesses in Jerusalem, and in all Judea and Samaria, and to the ends of the earth.*" Acts 1:8

Prayer – Lord, today I admit that Your ways are higher than I can fathom. You have asked me, with all my inconsistencies to be THE messenger of Your Good News. When I join with others in Your family, You empower us to touch the entire world with Your message.

Today, though I am one small piece, I commit to join Your work in the earth. I will not stop until every person, in every culture, in every nation has heard of You great love. In Jesus' name, Amen.

Day 30

A Destiny of PEACE

A Truth to Live – God empowers me to live and give His PEACE.

Scripture – *"Go and make disciples of all nations, baptizing them in the name of the Father and of the Son and of the Holy Spirit, and teaching them to obey everything I have commanded you."* Matthew 28:19

Prayer – Lord, I commit to live with Your destiny as my priority in life. I choose to view Your divine calling to go and tell the Good News and to make disciples to be of utmost importance in my life. I believe that You have supernaturally placed me in my family, with my friends, in my neighborhood and with colleagues at work for the specific purpose of sharing Your PEACE with them.

For the sake of Your name and Your glory, I commit to spend the rest of my days living in Your destiny for my life. I will:

Proclaim Your kingdom
Equip others to change their world
Assist the poor
Care for the sick
Educate the next generation

In Jesus' name, Amen.

Day 31

God Brings Order to Chaos

A Truth to Live – In the beginning, the very beginning, there was chaos, disorder and lifelessness. And then God "hovered" over the mess and brought order and beauty. The breath of God spoke life to brokenness and it came to be. God is the same today – He finds things that are broken and dysfunctional and brings healing and wholeness.

Scripture – *"In the beginning God created the heavens and the earth. Now the earth was formless and empty, darkness was over the surface of the deep, and the Spirit of God was hovering over the waters. And God said, "Let there be light," and there was light."* Genesis 1:1-3

Prayer – Heavenly Father, I come to You today, imperfect and troubled, but I am so grateful You will "hover" over my brokenness and bring healing to me. I ask that You would speak light and life into my being by the power of Your Spirit. In Jesus' name, Amen.

Day 32

God Brings Life to All Creation

A Truth to Live – God's Word is life-giving and hope-generating. From the beginning of time until now – and through tomorrow – the words of God will bring into being the goodness of His character and will showcase His love and mercy toward all of His creation.

Scripture – *"For the word of the Lord is right and true; he is faithful in all He does. The Lord loves righteousness and justice; the earth is full of His unfailing love. By the word of the Lord were the heavens made, their starry host by the breath of His mouth."* Psalms 33:4-6

Prayer – Heavenly Father, thank You for bringing life and hope to me. Through the power of Your words the heavens were made, and I ask today that You would speak Your words of life over me. Help me to trust You to be faithful to fill my life with Your unfailing love. In Jesus' name, Amen

Day 33

God Breathes Life in Me and Through Me

A Truth to Live – When God speaks His very breath has the power to bring everything to life, even the darkest part of your world. He is the one who made me, and His words will sustain me to live out what I was made for – to enjoy Him and His creation forever.

Scripture – *"The Spirit of God has made me; the breath of the Almighty gives me life."* Job 33:4

Prayer – Eternal Father, thank You for the power and gentleness of Your Spirit. Today, I acknowledge that You are the One who made me, who created me for good. Help me honor You today by living in a way that shares Your light and hope with others. In Jesus' name, Amen.

Day 34

God Fills Me with Purpose

A Truth to Live – God chose me, created me and handcrafted every part of my being with a unique blend of skills, abilities and knowledge. God designed me with a majestic and glorious purpose that will satisfy my deepest longing. He wants me to use what I have been given to glorify Him by acknowledging His imprint in my life.

Scripture – *"Then the Lord said to Moses, 'See I have chosen Bezalel and I have filled him with the Spirit of God, with skill, ability and knowledge in all kinds of crafts…"* Exodus 31:1-4

Prayer – Gracious Father, I thank You today that You chose me to fit into a larger and grander plan than what I can see. You have created me with skills and abilities that were designed to honor You and allow others to find hope in You. Help me today to use what I have been given to honor You. In Jesus' name, Amen.

Day 35

The Holy Spirit is Our Communion

A Truth to Live – God has designed my life to be surrounded, protected and guided by Him. To bridge the gap between where I am today and who He is in eternity, God has placed His Spirit to live within me and to provide the deepest and richest communion with Him.

Scripture – *"May the grace of the Lord Jesus Christ, and the love of God, and the fellowship of Holy Spirit be with you all."* 2 Corinthians 13:14

Prayer – Eternal God, You are beautiful beyond description. You have offered Your love to me, granted me eternal grace through Your Son, Jesus, and You have invited me to life with and in You through the gift of Your Spirit. Help me to treasure my day and to see the life-giving nature of Your Spirit in me. In Jesus' name, Amen.

Day 36

God's Love is Made Real to Me

A Truth to Live – God has made a way for me to understand His greatness, His kindness and His unending mercy for me. He designed the world, breathed life into my being and wants to remain in constant communion with me! Not only has He offered His saving grace through His Son, but He promises to pour out His love to me by the power of His Spirit!

Scripture – *"And hope does not disappoint us, because God has poured out His love into our hearts by the Holy Spirit, whom He has given us."* Romans 5:5

Prayer – Heavenly Father, thank You for generously giving me Your love and pouring it out in my heart by the power and nature of Your Holy Spirit. Help me to be attentive today to Your never-ending love and to receive Your healing and direction that comes from Your guidance. In Jesus' name, Amen.

Day 37

God Fills Me with Light and Life

A Truth to Live – God has created a path for me to walk from death to life. All of the hurts, pains, sorrows and troubles that weigh me down each day cannot over power the work of Jesus Christ and the presence of the Holy Spirit. God will breathe life into every person that follows Him!

Scripture – *"And if the Spirit of Him who raised Jesus from the dead is living in you, He who raised Christ from the dead will also give life to your mortal bodies through His Spirit, who lives in you."* Romans 8:11

Prayer – Eternal and All Powerful God, You are full of grace and mercy, and I thank You today for blessing me with eternal life. I receive the power and presence of Your Spirit to heal my brokenness, to restore my heart and to speak light and life in my being. Thank You! In Jesus' name, Amen.

Day 38

God Reveals Himself to Me

A Truth to Live – God knows that on my own it is impossible to understand the depth and riches of heaven, eternity and never ending love of God. But rather than leave me ignorant, God instead chooses to send me His Spirit to reveal His goodness, mercy and love!

Scripture – *"The man without the Spirit does not accept the things that come from the Spirit of God, for they are foolishness to him and he cannot understand them, because they are spiritually discerned."*
1 Corinthians 2:14

Prayer – Heavenly Father, thank You for providing Your abundant blessings and eternal love to me. I know that I can't possibly fathom the richness of Your love and forgiveness, or the fruit of Your Spirit and its power. Help me to rely on the revelation of Your Spirit today so that I can learn to know You more. In Jesus' name, Amen.

Day 39

God Teaches Me to Pray

A Truth to Live – God knows that in times of great victory and in the midst of trials there can be moments when I don't know how or what to pray. Fortunately, the Spirit of God has been placed in my heart and offers up prayers that are more powerful than words can express!

Scripture – *"the Spirit helps us in our weakness. We do not know what we ought to pray for, but the Spirit himself intercedes for us with groans that words cannot express. And he who searches our hearts knows the mind of the Spirit, because the Spirit intercedes for the saints in accordance with God's will."* Romans 8:26-27

Prayer – Heavenly Father, thank You for imparting to me Your Spirit. When I do not know how to pray, or what to say, I am confident that Your Spirit is interceding on my behalf offering prayers to You that will be heard in heaven. Help me to rely more on Your Spirit every day and to pray in the Spirit and with my understanding. In Jesus' name, Amen.

Day 40

God Reveals the Truth of His Word

A Truth to Live – God knows that my mind is finite and His ways are infinite. My view is limited and His is unlimited. Because of His great love for me and His desire for me to walk in wholeness and abundance, God has placed His Spirit inside of me to be the revealer of truth and the fountain of wisdom.

Scripture – *"I keep asking that the God of our Lord Jesus Christ, the glorious Father, may grant you the Spirit of wisdom and revelation, so that you may know him better."* Ephesians 1:17-18

Prayer – Heavenly Father, thank You for the gift of Your Spirit. You know that on my own I do not have the wisdom to make it through my day, or plan for tomorrow. Help me to depend on the supernatural wisdom of God and His revelation to chart my course and to direct my days. In Jesus' name, Amen.

Day 41

God Points Me in the Right Direction

A Truth to Live – God has sent me a Counselor and Guide to help me make the right choices. His Holy Spirit works to keep me walking on God's path, prompts me to make the wise choices and guides me toward His truth. When I follow the lead of the Holy Spirit I will discover the blessings of God's presence.

Scripture – *"But when the Spirit of truth comes, he will guide you into all truth."* John 16:7-11

Prayer – Gracious Father, thank You for the gift of Your Holy Spirit. He is my Counselor, my Guide and the Revealer of wisdom and truth. Today I give up control of my life and yield it to You. Direct my days by the power and truth of Your Spirit. In Jesus' name, Amen.

Day 42

God's Spirit Produces Good Spiritual Fruit

A Truth to Live – God wants me to know His Spirit is at work in me! When I allow the counsel and guidance of the Holy Spirit to direct my day it will produce an abundance of wholesome character, the strength to resist all evil and a countenance that glorifies God.

Scripture – *"The fruit of the Spirit is love, joy, peace, patience, kindness, goodness, faithfulness, gentleness and self-control. Since we live by the Spirit, let us keep in step with the Spirit."* Galatians 5:22-25

Prayer – Heavenly Father, today I commit to yield to the abundant counsel and wisdom revealed in my heart through the power of Your Spirit. Help me to resist the temptations that surround me and to allow Your Spirit to produce in me a character that blesses those around me and honors You. In Jesus' name, Amen.

Day 43

God Renews

A Truth to Live – God has the power to renew my heart, re-energize my spirit and give me confidence to walk humbly before Him each and every day. When my daily responsibilities and the commitment to live holy bring fatigue, God has promised that His Spirit has the power to renew.

Scripture – *"He saved us, not because of righteous things we have done, but because of His mercy. He saved us through the washing of rebirth and renewal by the Holy Spirit."* Titus 3:5

Prayer – Gracious Father, I ask that You renew me today. Strengthen my heart and restore joy to me and grant me the confidence to walk in the boldness of Your Spirit. I am dependent today on Your revelation and direction. In Jesus' name, Amen.

Day 44

God Anoints Me for Life, for Battle and for Victory

A Truth to Live – I was not created by accident. In fact, my purpose was forged in heaven and finds supernatural strength through the presence and power of the Holy Spirit. God promises to pour out His Spirit on me and to fulfill His work in my life.

Scripture – *"You have an anointing from the Holy One, and all of you know the truth."* 1 John 2:20

Prayer – Eternal Father, thank You today for the power of Your anointing. It pulls me up out of mediocrity; it strengthens my resolve, empowers me to worship You and directs my feet to walk in Your path. Draw me closer to You so that Your anointing overwhelms my insecurities and guides my steps. In Jesus' name.

Day 45

God Promises His Power

A Truth to Live – God knows that on my own I can't live a holy and pure life, nor take part in the miracles that He wants to perform around me and through me. That is why He promises to reside by His Spirit within me! When I receive the infilling of the Holy Spirit He gives me the supernatural power to do God's will on the earth.

Scripture – *"I am going to send you what my Father has promised, but stay in the city until you have been clothed with power from on high."* Luke 24:49

Prayer – Gracious Father, today I realize that much of my own Christian life is centered around the work that I do, the service I perform, or my own devotional prayer life. I am asking You to help re-orient my time with You to focus less on my own efforts and more on waiting for Your power to infuse every part of me. In Jesus' name, Amen.

Day 46

God Speaks Direction Into My Life

A Truth to Live – God knows that I have a tendency to stray from the path that He designed for me. Fortunately He has not left me alone, nor asked me to find my way by myself. He wants to lead me and guide me into all truth and to speak supernatural direction into my life.

Scripture – *"I am Jesus…now get up and go into the city, and you will be told what you must do."*
Luke 9:5-6

Prayer – Heavenly Father, thank You for the power of Your Spirit! Open my ears to hear the truth of Your voice so that I can follow Your path. I am waiting for You to instruct me in the paths of righteousness and to lead me each day to be a part of Your amazing plan. In Jesus' name, Amen.

Day 47

God Invites Me Into a Life of Miracles

A Truth to Live – God has miraculous plans for me that are better than any life goals or ambitions I could come with on my own. He wants to partner with me to carry out His purposes in the earth and to bring His miraculous and transforming power into the lives of those I love, to my friends and even to the nations of the earth.

Scripture – *"Silver or gold I do not have but what I have I give you. In the name of Jesus Christ of Nazareth, walk."* Acts 3:6

Prayer – Eternal Father, You are the God of all creation, and I am just a person living on Your earth. Help me to recognize that the incredible gift of Your Spirit is for the working of supernatural power, for healing and deliverance. Teach me to be a part of Your work in changing peoples' lives. In Jesus' name, Amen.

Day 48

God Gives Me the Power to Overcome Temptation

A Truth to Live – God has granted me supernatural power to overcome the temptations that confront me each and every day. When I choose to partner with Him, God will walk with me through every trial and circumstance, filling me with the truth of His Word and helping me to focus on His power to overcome evil.

Scripture – *"Jesus, full of the Holy Spirit, returned from the Jordan and was led by the Spirit in the desert..."* Luke 4:1

Prayer – Heavenly Father, thank You for the gift of Your Spirit. Help me to depend more on You each day – to lead me through times of great victory and to strengthen me through times of trial. Thank You for granting me the power of Your Spirit to overcome the temptation that is all around me. In Jesus' name, Amen.

Day 49

God Gives Me Power Over Demons

A Truth to Live – God is for me. He feels every wound, identifies with every broken heart and walks with me through every trial. He also knows that I have been placed in a spiritual battle against evil – and He has designed me to win! Through the power of His Spirit He grants me the power to overcome and defeat every demon power.

Scripture – *"When Jesus had called the twelve together, he gave them power and authority to drive out all demons and to cure diseases, and he sent them out to preach the kingdom of God and to heal the sick."* Luke 9:1-2

Prayer – Heavenly Father, today I choose to admit to You my own fears and pain. Rather than trying to manage my own shortcomings and hide them from others I will hand them to You. Help me to walk in the spiritual authority that You have given me and to destroy the work of the devil in my life. In Jesus' name, Amen.

Day 50

God Gives Me Power Over Sickness

A Truth to Live – God has chosen me to be an instrument of His glory and He wants to use my life as a witness of His amazing love, mercy and healing power. He has given me the power to stand against the evil attacks of sickness and disease and to not allow them to influence my spirit. He has given me the authority to heal.

Scripture – *"When Jesus had called the twelve together, he gave them power and authority to drive out all demons and to cure diseases, and he sent them out to preach the kingdom of God and to heal the sick."* Luke 9:1-2

Truth – Merciful Father, thank You for giving me the authority and power over sickness and disease! I admit that so often I put my trust in others and do not place You as the Healer in my life. I know that You can use, prayer, medicine, nutrition, time and many other means to bring my healing. Help me to walk confidently through my day, trusting You to be my Source of healing. In Jesus' name Amen.

Day 51

He Gives Joy

A Truth to Live – God knows that when circumstances suddenly change or words are exchanged my heart can be filled with sorrow. That is why His Spirit resides in me to become the source and supply of my being and a fountain of joy that will flow from my heart and give me reason to praise Him through every part of my day.

Scripture – *"At that time Jesus, full of joy through the Holy Spirit, said 'I praise you, Father, Lord of heaven and earth, because you have hidden these things from the wise and learned and revealed them to little children. Yes, Father, for this was your good pleasure."* Luke 10:21

Prayer – Eternal Father, today I turn to You as my source and supply of joy. When my day is disrupted or sadness comes at me help me to turn again to You, and allow Your Spirit to fill me with the eternal joy of Your Spirit. In Jesus' name, Amen.

Day 52

God Wants Me to Live in the Supernatural

A Truth to Live – God's greatest desire is to fulfill His mission through me! His plan for me includes my salvation, freedom from the bondage of sin and the power of His Spirit to live each day on mission for Him.

Scripture – *"All of them were filled with the Holy Spirit and began to speak in other tongues as the Spirit enabled them."* Acts 2:4

Prayer – Heavenly Father, today I ask that You would prepare my heart to live supernaturally for You. I realize that for too long I have focused my faith on what I can do for You, and now I understand that You want to fill me with the power of Your Spirit and fuel me with Your supernatural gifts. I receive Your gift! In Jesus' name, Amen.

Day 53

God Wants to Show Himself to Me

A Truth to Live – God is for me, and He wants me to be infused with the revelation of His goodness and the power to supernaturally see His purposes at work in the whole earth. The expectation of godly visions, word-based prophecies, and glory-filled unknown tongues are not only something from the past – they are part of God's way of revealing Himself to me.

Scripture – *"In the last days, God says, I will pour out my Spirit on all people. Your sons and daughters will prophesy, your young men will see visions, your old men will dream dreams."* Acts 2:17-18

Prayer – Eternal God, thank You for sending Your Spirit to me. I ask that today You would show Yourself to me with dreams and visions of Your purposes, with prophetic words and with unknown tongues that will declare Your praises. Help me to step out of my comfort zone and allow You to use me. In Jesus' name, Amen.

Day 54

God Wants Me to See and Hear His Spirit

A Truth to Live – Once and for all God has revealed Himself, His purposes and His plan to all people. There are no secrets. He wants to reveal to me His goodness, have me understand His salvation, and experience the power of His Spirit and His future for me.

Scripture – *"Exalted to the right hand of God, he has received from the Father the promised Holy Spirit and has poured out what you now see and hear."*
Acts 2:33

Prayer – Heavenly Father, thank You for bringing the power of the Holy Spirit to me. I am grateful that You have openly demonstrated His actions in the Scripture, and I ask now that what I read in Your Word I would experience in my life. In Jesus' name, Amen.

Day 55

God Wants to Refresh Me By His Spirit

A Truth to Live – God knows that the trials and circumstances of life can wear me down and drain my joy, so He has provided the presence of His Spirit to renew and restore my body, mind and spirit. He wants to refresh me today!

Scripture – *"Repent, then, and turn to God so that your sins may be wiped out, that times of refreshing may come from the Lord."* Acts 3:19

Prayer – Gracious Father, thank You for loving me so much that You desire to refresh every part of my being. Today I turn from going my own way, and instead choose to follow You. I know that in doing so, I will be freed from my sin and will experience Your refreshing Spirit. Refresh me, Lord. In Jesus' name, Amen.

Day 56

God Wants Me to be a Part of His Healing Power

A Truth to Live – God's purpose for me includes much more than living out my "destiny" or using the "gifts" that He has given me. God desires to use me to pray for healing and perform miraculous signs and wonders in His name. He want me to be a part of living His supernatural life!

Scripture – *"Stretch out your hand to heal and perform miraculous signs and wonders through the name of your holy servant Jesus. After they prayed, the place where they were meeting was shaken. And they were all filled with the Holy Spirit and spoke the word of God boldly."* Acts 4:30-31

Prayer – Heavenly Father, today I ask You to operate Your supernatural gifts through me. Use me to heal the sick and to perform mighty miracles in Your name. I will speak boldly for You. In Jesus' name, Amen.

Day 57

God Wants Me to be a Part of His Miracles

A Truth to Live – God has promised to pour out His Spirit on all flesh – on everyone, and He wants to use me to bring the supernatural power of His message to my world. He will equip me with boldness, the words to say and powerful prayers to bring His healing to the broken and to see miracles happen.

Scripture – *"Go to the house of Judas on Straight Street and ask for a man from Tarsus named Saul, for he is praying. In a vision he has seen [you] a man come and place his hands on him to restore his sight."* Acts 9:10-16

Prayer – Gracious Father, today I come to You and thank You for granting to me the power to join You in reaching my world with the glory of Your name, the power of forgiveness and the supernatural presence of Your Spirit. Teach me to listen for Your direction and to walk in confidence so that I can boldly see You work in the lives of those around me. In Jesus' name, Amen.

Day 58

God Wants Me to Receive His Spirit

A Truth to Live – God wants me to receive the supernatural blessings of His Spirit. Just as the early disciples were blessed on the day of Pentecost, God wants to bless me. His plans for me include the supernatural. God wants to bless my world through me!

Scripture – *"Can anyone keep these people from being baptized? They have received the Holy Spirit just was we have."* Acts 10:47

Prayer – Gracious Heavenly Father, today I yield to the overwhelming love that You have poured out in my life. I know that You want to fill me with Your Spirit so that I overflow and become a supernatural blessing to those around me. I am ready for You to pour out Your Spirit in my life! In Jesus' name, Amen.

Day 59

God Wants to Lead Me by His Spirit

A Truth to Live – God's Spirit is at work in the hearts of people all over the earth. He is preparing them for the Good News of the Gospel and to receive salvation through His Son Jesus Christ. Now, He wants to lead me, very specifically, to the people who hunger for Him. It is a partnership of supernatural proportions.

Scripture – *"When Paul and Silas came to the border of Mysia, they tried to enter Bithynia, but the Spirit of Jesus would not allow them to. During the night Paul had a vision of a man from Macedonia standing and begging him, 'Come over and help us.' After Paul had seen the vision, we got ready at once to leave... concluding that God had called us to preach the Gospel to them."* Acts 16:7-10

Prayer – Heavenly Father, I ask that You would baptize me with Your Spirit. Grant to me visions and dreams of Your plan for my life, and fill me with supernatural wisdom to follow Your direction. In Jesus' name, Amen.

Day 60

God Wants to Empower Me

A Truth to Live – God's intentions for my life reach far beyond what I can see or imagine. His destiny for me begins with an infusion of His power and then continues with me walking in His supernatural abundance. He wants my words to operate in supernatural power.

Scripture – *"Did you receive the Holy Spirit when you believed?"* Acts 19:2

Prayer – Eternal God, I ask for an infilling of the power of Your Spirit today. Baptize me with fire, renew my passion and zeal for You and fill my mouth with supernatural wisdom, prophecy, languages I don't know and revelations beyond my understanding! In Jesus' name, Amen.

Day 61

God Wants to Live Through Me

Truth – God has a specific plan for my life that includes living and operating in the supernatural power of His Spirit. He has not left me to journey through life in your own strength, but instead is passionate about living through me by His Spirit. God wants to live through me.

Scripture – *"And now, compelled by the Holy Spirit, I am going to Jerusalem."* Acts 20:22

Prayer – Heavenly Father, I read the words of Your Scripture today, and I ask You to help me to hear Your voice and to be compelled to do Your will. I know that my heart will hunger and never be satisfied until I am being used in supernatural ways to bless Your world. In Jesus' name, Amen.

Day 62

Jesus Turns Water into Wine

A Truth to Live to Live – Whenever I find myself in a bind, in trouble or facing circumstances that affect my well-being I know there is an answer. When I invite Jesus to take over my world He always provides the solutions to my need.

Scripture – *"Jesus said, 'Fill the ceremonial jars with water...draw some out and take it to the master of the banquet.' They did so and the master of the banquet tasted the water that had been turned into wine. He said to the bridegroom... 'you have saved the best wine till now!'"* John 2:1-11

Prayer – Heavenly Father, I admit today that the difficulties I am in are too big for me to solve. Rather than give up, or live in fear, I am handing You what seems empty, asking You to fill it, and trusting by faith that You will meet my every need. In Jesus name, Amen.

Day 63

Take Jesus at His Word

A Truth to Live – Jesus always fulfills His promise. I can trust that when I bring my deepest need to Jesus He is there to listen, to act and to do what is right. He is faithful to comfort, to heal, to deliver and to see His Word fulfilled.

Scripture – *"When the royal official heard that Jesus had arrived…he went to him and begged him to come and heal his son, who was close to death. The official said, 'Sir, come down before my child dies.' Jesus replied, 'You may go, your son will live. The man took Jesus at His word and departed."* John 4:46-54

Prayer – Jesus, I will take You at Your Word. What you say is true, faithful and unchanging. When You speak to me it is all that I need. I know You will accomplish what You say. I trust You. In Your Holy name, Amen.

Day 64

Jesus Makes Demons Flee

A Truth to Live – Evil is real. Evil spirits attach themselves to people and wreak havoc in their lives. But even demons know they have met their match when they are faced with Jesus of Nazareth. He has the power to cast out demons.

Scripture – *"In the synagogue there was a man possessed by a demon, an evil spirit. He cried out at the top of his voice, 'Ha! What do you want with us, Jesus of Nazareth? Have you come to destroy us? I know who you are – the Holy One of God.' 'Be quiet!' Jesus said sternly. 'Come out of him.' ...and the spirit came out without injuring the man."* Luke 4:31-37

Prayer – Father, many times I pretend that evil is not real and that it has no impact on my life. But, today I know that You are more powerful than every demon from hell; You are mightier than evil itself. Set me free today from the chains of evil and place Your protective authority over me. In Jesus' name, Amen.

Day 65

Jesus Has Authority over Sickness

A Truth to Live – There is a feeling of hopelessness that can settle over me when I am sick. It is a sense that I am powerless to overcome its devastation. Jesus has compassion on those who are sick and heals them!

Scripture – *"Simon's mother-in-law was suffering from a high fever, and they asked Jesus to help her. So he bent over her and rebuked the fever and it left her. She got up at once!"* Luke 4:38-39

Prayer – Jesus, today my prayer is very simple. Can You come near to me and help me? I need Your healing. And for those that I know who are sick, rebuke their illness with the authority and power of Your name, Jesus. Amen.

Day 66

Jesus Provides

A Truth to Live – Panic can easily set in when provision seems scarce. However, God provides a remedy to overcome the barriers of lack; it is to call on the Creator and Source of all wealth. God promises His followers the power to create wealth (Deuteronomy 8:18).

Scripture – *"Jesus said, 'Put out into deep [unknown] water, and let down the nets for a catch.' Simon answered, 'Master, we've worked hard all night and haven't caught anything. But because you say so, I will let down the nets.' When they had done so, they caught such a large number of fish that their nets began to break."* Luke 5:3-10

Prayer – Jesus, You know what I need today. You see past my feeble attempts and uselessness of my own efforts. I ask for Your revelation and wisdom to guide me toward obedience and abundance. In Jesus' name, Amen.

Day 67

Jesus is Able and Always Willing

A Truth to Live – When the stranglehold of sickness, disease, trouble and pain saps the life out of me it is easy to dim my vision and lower my expectations of Jesus. Sometimes I can even wonder if He is still willing to rescue me. He is!

Scripture – *"A man with leprosy came and knelt before him and said, 'Lord if you are willing, you can make me clean.' Jesus reached out his hand and touched the man. 'I am willing,' he said. 'Be clean." Immediately he was cured of leprosy."* Matthew 8:1-3

Prayer – God, I know You are able to do anything. You created the universe and everything in it. But, honestly, sometimes I need to know that You are willing to help me. Help me to trust the power of Your Word and allow Your truth to make me brand new. In Jesus' name, Amen.

Day 68

Jesus' Words Have the Power to Heal

A Truth to Live – Circumstances have a strange way of dominating my thoughts and organizing my conduct. Stress, pressure, pain, sickness, disease and trouble can act as blinders to the reality that the words of Jesus always speak life and deliverance to my heart and mind.

Scripture – *"A soldier came to Jesus asking for help. 'Lord,' he said, 'my servant lies at home paralyzed and in terrible suffering. Jesus said, 'I will go and heal him.' The soldier replied, 'Lord I do not deserve to have you come under my roof. But just say the word, and my servant will be healed. Then Jesus said, 'Go! It will be done just as you believed it would."*
Matthew 8:5-13

Prayer – Heavenly Father, thank You for promising to help me. I know that You see my troubled state and will always come to my rescue. Today I ask that You would speak to me by the power of Your Word and the gentleness of Your Spirit. I will trust in You. In Jesus, name, Amen.

Day 69

Jesus Responds to Faith

A Truth to Live – Sometimes the physical and emotional pain of my past can prevent me from entering a promising future. It is in these moments that I need a faith-filled support structure that will bring me to Jesus. He has the power to heal!

Scripture – *"Some men brought Jesus a paralytic…and when Jesus saw their faith, he said the paralytic, 'Take heart, son; your sins are forgiven [and then] get up, and take your mat and go home."* Matthew 9:1-8

Prayer – Heavenly Father, find me today and deliver me from the bondage of my past. I ask that You surround me with believing friends who would insure that I depend only on You to be my deliverer and healer. In Jesus' name, Amen.

Day 70

Jesus Always Restores

A Truth to Live – People who depend on their own works to earn a "place" with God always fall short. But Jesus always looks beyond religious rituals to find willing hearts that are open to His intervention and miraculous touch.

Scripture – *"Jesus went into the synagogue, and a man with a shriveled hand was there. [The Pharisees] asked, 'is it lawful to heal on the Sabbath?' He said to them, 'It is lawful to do good on the Sabbath.' He said to the man, 'Stretch out your hand.' So he stretched it out and it was completely restored, just as sound as the other."* Matthew 12:9-14

Prayer – Heavenly Father, I am grateful that You are a healer. Help me to push beyond my own self-imposed rules and obey and follow You. I know that I will find healing when I obey Your Word. In Jesus' name, Amen.

Day 71

Jesus Raises the Dead

A Truth to Live – Jesus is the beginning and the end of all things. He is Life. He is Hope and He is Forever. Jesus is the only one who can breathe life into what others have declared to be dead.

Scripture – *"As Jesus approached the town gate, a dead person was being carried out – the only son of his mother, and she was a widow. Jesus went up and touched the coffin and said, 'Young man, I say to you get up!' The dead man sat up and began to talk and Jesus gave him back to His mother."* Luke 7:11-17

Prayer – Gracious and Life-giving Father, today I ask that You would breathe life in to me. Place me in circumstances where my faith will be stretched to see You bring those things that are dead back to life. I believe in You. In Jesus' name, Amen.

Day 72

Jesus Promises to Get Me to the Other Side

A Truth to Live – When the obstacles, issues and problems in front of me are too big for me to overcome I can count on the reality that Jesus is Sovereign and that nothing is impossible with Him (Matthew 19:26). Being with Him insures my safe passage to the other side!

Scripture – *"A furious squall came up, the waves broke over the boat and it was nearly swamped. Jesus was in the stern, sleeping. The disciples woke him and said, 'Teacher, don't you care if we drown?' He got up, rebuked the wind and said to the waves, 'Quiet! Be still!' Then the wind died down and it was completely calm."* Mark 4:35-41

Prayer – Heavenly Father, thank You for sending the Reigning King into my life. I know that He is with me, today. Help me not to panic when obstacles seem too large to overcome or when issues try to paralyze my future. Instead, teach me to place my faith in You. In Jesus' name, Amen.

Day 73

Jesus Has Power Over Evil

A Truth to Live – The violence and pain of evil can work their way into my life; steal my joy and, at times, render me completely useless. But even the grip of evil has no power in the presence of Jesus, the Savior. When I cling to Jesus evil has no power!

Scripture – "*Two demon-possessed men coming from the tombs met Him. They were so violent that no one could pass that way. 'What do you want with us, Son of God?' they shouted. 'Have you come here to torture us before the appointed time?' Then he said to the demons, 'GO' and they left the men…*"
Luke 8:28-34

Prayer – Omnipotent and Eternal Father, I realize that the impact of evil and pain has numbed my heart and deadened my desire to live for You. I am helpless without the power of Your Son Jesus. I ask that You would command all evil to leave me, now and forever. In Jesus' name, Amen.

Day 74

Jesus Heals

A Truth to Live – Desperation is a strong motivation. When I feel pressed against a wall, or my heart is broken to pieces, I am confronted with a choice: self-preservation or surrender. The first option depends on my strength, the second on the healing power of Jesus!

Scripture – *"Just then a woman who had been subject to bleeding for 12 years came up and touched the edge of his cloak. She said to herself, 'If I only touch His cloak, I will be healed.' Jesus turned and saw her. "Take heart, daughter,' He said, 'your faith has healed you.' And the woman was healed from that moment."* Matthew 9:20-22

Prayer – Merciful God, rescue me today from the sickness and disease that plagues my mind and my body. I have faith that You are more powerful than the issues that face me, and I expect to be healed when You touch me. In Jesus' name, Amen.

Day 75

With Jesus It's Never Over

A Truth to Live – When I think that I can fix it, solve it, repair it or change it, then I take the matter out of Jesus' hands and into my own. But when I hand everything to Jesus He has the power to speak life even into the darkest corners of death.

Scripture – *"A ruler came and knelt before Jesus and said, 'My daughter has just died. But come and put your hand on her, and she will live.' When Jesus' entered the ruler's house He spoke to the funeral procession and said, 'Go away. The girl is not dead but asleep.' But they laughed at Him. After the crowd had been put outside, He went in and took the girl by the hand and she got up."* Matthew 9:18-19, 23-26

Prayer – Gracious Father, I come to You in faith, believing that Your Son Jesus is the Beginning and the End. He knows all, sees all and has power over all. When He speaks to my situation life will come! Even when others laugh I will not yield from the love of my Savior. In Jesus' name, Amen.

Day 76

Jesus Asks if I Believe

A Truth to Live – Facing a problem or difficulty? There is no lack of ability or willingness on Jesus' part. He remains willing to do a miracle on my behalf, but He wants to know if I believe that He can and will. Jesus will respond to your faith in Him.

Scripture – *"The blind men came to Him and he asked them, 'Do you believe that I am able to [heal]?' 'Yes Lord,' they replied. Then He touched their eyes and said, 'According to your faith will it be done to you'; and their sight was restored."* Matthew 9:27-31

Prayer – Heavenly Father, thank You for sending Your Son, Jesus, to carry out Your mission of love, forgiveness, salvation, healing and restoration. Help me today to point my faith toward You and not toward my own abilities. I believe that You can and will heal. In Jesus' name, Amen.

Day 77

Jesus Gives Speech to the Mute

A Truth to Live – Jesus has power over life and death; darkness and light; good and evil; sickness and health; even the evil of demonic power. Do I have a problem too big for me to solve? Remember, there is nothing impossible with God (Luke 18:27).

Scripture – "*A man who was demon-possessed and could not talk was brought to Jesus. And when the demon was driven out [by Jesus], the man who had been mute spoke. The crowd was amazed and said, 'Nothing like this have ever been in Israel.'*" Matthew 9:32-33

Prayer – Heavenly Father, You have given Your Son power over life and death and the evil of this world. I place my confidence in You today that you will free me from bondage and give me words to declare Your glory. In Jesus' name, Amen.

Day 78

Jesus Waits for Me

A Truth to Live – The Creator of the Universe deployed His only Son to earth for the specific mission of destroying the works of evil (John 3:8) and bringing new life to all who follow Him. When I am faced with a broken past, or paralyzed by the present, Jesus is ready to deliver me from darkness to light!

Scripture – *"When Jesus saw [the invalid] lying there and learned that he had been in this condition for a long time, He asked him, 'Do you want to get well?' 'Sir,' the invalid replied, 'I have no one to help me…' Then Jesus said to him, 'Get up! Pick up your mat and walk."* John 5:5-17

Prayer – God, You are full of grace and truth. I come to you today, riddled from the impact of evil and the poor choices I have made. I feel trapped. But I am asking Your Son, Jesus, to speak the words so that I can be healed and restored to the purpose You have for me. In Jesus' name, Amen.

Day 79

Jesus Asks Me to Join Him in Doing Miracles

A Truth to Live – Jesus can see every need I have; all those around me and even those I can't see. Because He is God's beloved Son, He knows what it takes to bring a miracle my way. The best news is that He invites me to join Him in miraculously meeting those needs!

Scripture – *"Jesus welcomed them and spoke to them about the Kingdom of God, and healed those who needed healing. Late in the afternoon the disciples said, 'Send the crowd away so they…can find food.' He replied, 'You give them something to eat.' They answered, 'We have only five loaves of bread and two fish.' He [took this food], gave thanks, broke them. Then he gave them to the disciples and all 5000 people were satisfied."* Luke 9:12-17

Prayer – Heavenly Father, thank You for inviting me to join Your Son Jesus in doing Your work. I choose today to stop looking at my own supply and start depending on You as the Source to meet the needs of all those I see. You are able, and I will follow You. In Jesus' name, Amen.

Day 80

Jesus Will Meet Me

A Truth to Live – Jesus never asks me to face the challenges of life by myself. When He commissions me into His work, He promises to be with me at all times. Even when times get rough and the seas are stormy, I will never walk alone.

Scripture – *"When evening came, the boat was in the middle of the lake…He saw the disciples straining at the oars, because the wind was with them. He went out to them, walking on the lake. When the disciples saw Him they were terrified. Immediately He spoke to them and said, 'Take courage, It is I. Don't be afraid." Then He climbed into the boat with them and the wind died down."* Mark 6:45-52

Prayer – Heavenly Father, when the storms of life seem to overwhelm me I will trust in Your Son to rescue me. I know that Jesus is able to be with me in my trouble and to end every trial that I face. I will trust in You! In Jesus' name, Amen.

Day 81

Jesus Respects Tenacious Faith

A Truth to Live – Jesus knows that the circumstances of life can weigh me down. His heart is for me, and He wants to be sure that I am willing to place all of my trust in Him. Sometimes He tests my allegiance and my tenacity to see if the loyalty of my heart will overpower the pressures of life.

Scripture – *"'Lord, Son of David, have mercy on me! My daughter is suffering terribly from demon-possession.' The woman came and knelt before Him. 'Lord, help me!' she said.' [Jesus tested her in conversation, but she pursued Him.] Then Jesus answered, 'Woman, you have great faith! Your request is granted'."* Matthew 15:21-28

Prayer – Heavenly Father, have mercy on me today. I am asking that You would work a miracle in my life through Your Son Jesus. I need to be free, and I believe You will do it! In Jesus' name, Amen.

Day 82

Jesus Heals!

A Truth to Live – Jesus responds to the faith and love of His followers. When I or someone I love is experiencing pain and suffering, I can turn to Him for answers. He will touch me right where I need it and make me whole!

Scripture – *"There some people brought to him a man who was deaf and could hardly talk, and they begged him to place His hand on the man. Jesus put his finger into the man's ears. Then he spit and touched the man's tongue. He looked up to heaven and with a deep sigh said to him, 'Be opened'."* Mark 7:31-37

Prayer – Gracious Father, I trust in the saving power of Your Son Jesus. I come to You today, bringing You my needs, and I ask You to touch me and make me whole! In Jesus' name, Amen.

Day 83

Jesus Always Completes What He Starts

A Truth to Live – When I have a hard time seeing where I am headed, I can find my way by trusting completely in Jesus. Jesus cares. And He takes the time to make sure that I know He has both the love and the power to bring wholeness and completeness in my life.

Scripture – [*Jesus] took the blind man by the hand and led him outside the village. When he had spit on the man's eyes and put His hands on him, Jesus asked, 'Do you see anything?' 'I see people; they look like trees walking around.' Once more Jesus put his hands on the man's eyes. Then his eyes were opened."* Mark 8:22-26

Prayer – Heavenly Father, how grateful I am today that You always complete the work that You begin (Phil 1:6). Rescue me today from being halfway – halfway healed, repaired and restored. Finish Your work in me so that others will glorify You. In Jesus Name, Amen.

Day 84

Jesus Makes Everything Possible

A Truth to Live – When evil wreaks its havoc, tossing me around and destroying everything in its path it is easy to lose hope and become discouraged. But Jesus makes all the difference. One word from Him will set me free from the grip of darkness.

Scripture – *"Jesus asked the boy's father, 'How long has he been like this?' 'From childhood,' he answered. The demon has often thrown him into the fire or water to kill him. But if you can do anything, take pity on us and help us. 'You deaf and mute spirit,' He said, 'I command you to come out of him and never enter him again.'"* Mark 9:14-29

Prayer – Jesus, I come to You today in complete desperation. I do not have the ability to rescue myself, but I believe that You can deliver me from evil. I ask You to command evil to leave my being right now and to never return. In Jesus' name, Amen.

Day 85

Jesus Has the Power

A Truth to Live – Jesus has the power over every circumstance, every situation, every influence, every issue and all the authority. There is nothing in heaven above or on earth below that is not under His feet or out of His reach.

Scripture – *"The tax collectors came to Peter and asked, 'Doesn't your teacher pay the temple tax?' Jesus said, 'Go to the lake and throw out your line. Take the first fish you catch, open its mouth and you will find a coin. Take it and give it to them for my tax and yours'."* Matthew 17:24-27

Prayer – Eternal God, You are the Creator and You have given Jesus, Your eternal Son, power over every man-made structure, government and entity. Teach me to honor Him above all else and to trust Him to meet my every need. In Jesus name, Amen.

Day 86

Jesus Has the Power Over Evil

A Truth to Live – The tragedies of life can bring discouragement, and evil and her tormenting spirits can cripple someone's life. But since Jesus has the authority in heaven and earth there is always hope. One simple word from Him can change my world!

Scripture – *"Jesus was teaching in the synagogue and a woman was there who had been crippled by a spirit for 18 years. She was bent over and could not straighten up at all. Jesus called her forward and said to her, 'Woman you are set free from your infirmity.' Then He put her hands on her and immediately she straightened up and praised God."* Luke 10:10-13

Prayer – Jesus, You alone can make me whole! You can set me free. It doesn't matter how long I have suffered or how complex my issue is, You can transform me today, right now. I place my life in Your hands, and I trust You to heal me. In Jesus' name, Amen.

Day 87

Jesus Sees Me as His Priority

A Truth to Live – There are many expectations and rules that others place on me. Even if their original intent was life-giving, many times the rules become the focus rather than the guide, and they become a hindrance to our healing.

Scripture – *"There was a man suffering from dropsy. Jesus asked the Pharisees and experts in the law, 'Is it lawful to heal on the Sabbath?' But they remained silent. So taking hold of the man, He healed him"* Luke 14:1-6

Prayer – Jesus, today I come to You knowing that I have allowed very well intentioned rules and traditions to be my focus. Help me to realize that You are my Source for healing, hope and restoration. In Jesus' name, Amen.

Day 88

Jesus Demands Obedience

A Truth to Live – Sometimes my predicaments and difficulties are caused because I live in a broken world. Other times I suffer because of evil or as a result of unwise decisions. Jesus has the power to heal and restore, and He demands complete obedience.

Scripture – *"As he was going to a village, ten men who had leprosy met him. They stood at a distance and called out in a loud voice, 'Jesus, Master, have pity on us.' When He saw them, He said, 'Go show yourselves to the priests.' And as they went, they were healed."* Luke 17:11-19

Prayer – Eternal and Gracious Father, today I come to You knowing that You are all powerful and able to heal. Help my response to You be to remain faithful and obedient so that I will not hinder Your work in my life. In Jesus' name, Amen.

Day 89

Jesus Has All Power

A Truth to Live – When darkness, discouragement or even the finality of death overwhelm me, I can take comfort and gain confidence in Jesus. He has the power over death, hell, the grave, sin, and every malady. He is God, and He is committed to rescue those who put their trust in Him.

Scripture – "*So the sisters sent word to Jesus, 'Lord, the one You love is sick.' When He heard this, Jesus said, 'This sickness will not end in death. It is for God's glory so that God's Son may be glorified through it.*" John 11:1-44

Prayer – Omnipotent and Eternal Father, You are ever powerful, and not even death can trap You. Today I cling to Your life-giving Spirit and ask that You would position me to give You glory. Speak to every dead part in my being and bring it to life. In Jesus' name, Amen.

Day 90

Jesus Shows Mercy

A Truth to Live – God created the world beautiful and good. But the sinful choices of humankind have filled it with self-focused endeavors, evil perpetrators, sickness, disease, tragedy, pain and brokenness. The reason God sent His only Son to earth was to destroy the works of evil (John 3:8) and to demonstrate His mercy toward me!

Scripture – *"When blind Bartimaeus heard that Jesus of Nazareth was passing by, he began to shout, 'Jesus, Son of David, have mercy on me!' 'What do you want me to do for you?' Jesus asked him. The blind man said, 'Rabbi, I want to see.' 'Go,' said Jesus, 'your faith has healed you'."* Mark 10:46-52

Prayer – Jesus, I am grateful today for Your never-ending mercy. Like the blind man on the side of the road I am calling out for You to heal me and make me see. Help me to point my faith toward You. In Jesus' name, Amen.

Day 91

Jesus Has Compassion

A Truth to Live – Doing the right thing is God's way. Even when the results could be detrimental, hurt or cause sorrow God is never evil and never succumbs to the temptation to do wrong. He is righteousness and is always filled with compassion toward me.

Scripture – *"When Jesus' followers saw [that He was going to be betrayed], they said, 'Lord shall we strike with our swords?' And one of them struck the servant of the high priest, cutting off his right ear. But Jesus answered, 'No more of this!' And He touched the man's ear and healed him."* Luke 22:47-51

Prayer – Eternal Father, today I admit that my instincts are not right. I often want to repay evil for evil and to make sure that my own reputation is defended. Help me to hear Your words, 'No more of this!' and to be filled with compassion. In Jesus' Name, Amen.

Day 92

Jesus Provides

A Truth to Live – People are creatures of habit. I like doing the familiar and feel comfortable repeating what I know. But God's provision often requires a move toward the unknown and a step of complete obedience toward Him.

Scripture – *"Early in the morning, Jesus stood on the shore, but the disciples did not realize it was Jesus. He called out to them, 'Friends, haven't you any fish?' 'No,' they answered. He said, 'Throw your net on the right side of the boat and you will find some.' When they did, they were unable to haul the net in because of the large number of fish."* John 21:4-11

Prayer – Jesus, I trust you. You know that I do better with routines and following a pattern in life. But I want to learn to trust You more than the pattern. Help me today to turn my focus toward the power of Your Word and expect a miracle provision. In Jesus' name, Amen.

Day 93

God Designed Me Before I Was Born

A Truth to Live – God has special plans for me. He created me in my mother's womb, saw me as my body was being formed and knit me together for an amazing purpose. Every single day of my life has spiritual destiny that honors God and provides total fulfillment.

Scripture – *"For you created my inmost being; you knit me together in my mother's womb. I praise you because I am fearfully and wonderfully made…your eyes saw my unformed body. All the days ordained for me were written in your book before one of them came to be."* Psalms 139:13-17

Prayer – Eternal and Everlasting God, You are my Creator, the great designer of my mind, my soul and my body. You have laid out for me a path to walk, a plan to live by and given me a heart to glorify Your Name. Help me today to live for You. In Jesus' name, Amen.

Day 94

Comparing Myself With Others is Foolish

A Truth to Live – God made me to honor Him, and it gives Him great pleasure to work through me. When I compare myself with others rather than the truth of God's Word confusion sets in; and foolishness, not wisdom, becomes my daily god. God loves what he made – me!

Scripture – *"We do not dare to classify or compare ourselves with some who commend themselves. When they measure themselves by themselves and compare themselves with themselves, they are not wise."* 2 Corinthians 10:12

Prayer – Eternal Wise God, You have made me perfect in Your eyes and designed my heart, my motives and my actions to live for You. Please help me today to not fall into the foolish distractions of comparison or an over emphasis on self-analysis. I will choose instead to worship You, to honor and respect the incredible works of Your hands. In Jesus' name, Amen

Day 95

God Has Given Me Purpose

A Truth to Live – God has charted a daily path for me. It is filled with the richness of His presence and guarantee of His goodness being used to re-create my life into something better, more beautiful and valuable. God turns everything for good!

Scripture – *"And we know that in all things God works for the good of those who love Him, who have been called according to His purpose. For those God foreknew He also predestined to be conformed to the likeness of His Son. And those He predestined, He also called; those He called, He also justified; those He justified, He also glorified."* Romans 8:28-30

Prayer – Heavenly Father, I give You thanks for the good plans that You have for me. You have crafted my days, designed my future and, by following You, I can have confidence that my spirit will be cleansed, strengthened made pure to honor You. Thank You for working in all things for my good. In Jesus' name, Amen

Day 96

God's Grace is at Work in Me

A Truth to Live – God knows that on my own life can be a lifeless struggle, and that is why He freely gives His grace to all those who follow Him. It is by His grace that I am saved in His Son, Jesus. It is by grace that I grow in Him, follow His path and live for Him. His grace is an amazing gift that empowers me to live for Him and pleasure in Him.

Scripture – *"But by the grace of God I am what I am and His grace to me was not without effect"...for it is God who works in you to will and to act according to His good purpose."* 1 Corinthians 15:10, Philippians 2:13

Prayer – Gracious Father, today I place my hopes and dreams in Your hands. I know that the gift of Your saving grace comes to me through Your Son, Jesus, and I receive the new life that He offers. Help me, Lord, to operate by and through Your grace and not in my own strength. In Jesus' name, Amen.

Day 97

God Shows His Power in My Weakness

A Truth to Live – God knows just what I need. His gifts are good, fruitful and lasting. There are "mountaintop" times of bounty and blessings, and God uses those for His glory. There are other "valley" moments that expose my inabilities, weaknesses and sufferings. God uses these moments to showcase His strength.

Scripture – *"To keep me from becoming conceited because of these surpassing great revelations, there was given me a thorn in the flesh, a messenger of Satan, to torment me. Three times I pleaded with the Lord to take it away from me. But He said, 'My grace is sufficient for you, for my power is made perfect in weakness'."* 1 Corinthians 12:7-10

Prayer – Eternal God, You are strong and filled with goodness. I am thankful that You have chosen to use my own shortcomings as points where Your grace can be strong. Help me to increase my dependence on You so that even when I am weak, I can be strong in You. In Jesus' name, Amen.

Day 98

God Gave Me a Spiritual Gift

A Truth to Live – God is the one who gives spiritual gifts. I have been given a very special spiritual gift from God that can only be activated through His grace given to me at salvation. The Good News is this: when I receive His free gift of grace He gives me the power to be His child and use His gifts to glorify Him every day of my life.

Scripture – *"But to each one of us grace gifts have been given as Christ apportioned it…[so that we might be equipped] and so that the body of Christ might be built up until we all reach unity in the faith and in the knowledge of the Son of God."* Ephesians 4:7,11-13; 1 Peter 4:10

Prayer – Gift-giving Eternal Father, thank You for Your eternal gifts that have no end. You have given me salvation through the work of Your Son on the cross, new life and the power to overcome evil with good. At the same time, Your daily grace brightens my day with joy and offers me gifts to bless others in Your name. I will praise You and use the gifts You have given me to make You known. In Jesus' name, Amen.

Day 99

God is Building Something Beautiful in Me

A Truth to Live – God has placed a unique value on me. Those around me may have more important roles, or super talents, but to God everyone is equally important to His good plan and can be used for His glory. God's gifts are all good, and they fit together so that we belong to one another and glorify Him with our love and deeds.

Scripture – *"God has combined the members of the body and has given greater honor to the parts that lacked it, so that there should be no division in the body, but that its parts should have equal concern for one another."* 1 Corinthians 12:21-26

Prayer – Heavenly Father, I praise You today for holding the whole universe together and for crafting Your plan through imperfect people like me! Thank You for the privilege of being used to share Your love with others and to help them see the value that You place on each of us – large or small, popular or unnoticed. I will honor You today. In Jesus' name, Amen.

Day 100

God has the Power to Forgive and Cleanse

A Truth to Live – God alone can take my deepest wounds and make them whole. He can wash my dark sins away and make me pure as the white snow. God, who shaped the human heart, has the power to forgive and cleanse every mistake, poor decision, and evil act I have ever committed. He is good and wants to extend His goodness to me.

Scripture – *"If we confess our sins, He is faithful and just and will forgive us our sins and purify us from all unrighteousness."* 1 John 1:9

Prayer – Gracious Heavenly Father, I come to You today with a heart full of mistakes, mis-starts, unfilled promises and dashed dreams. Thank You for receiving me just as I am. I confess my sins to You now and ask that You would forgive me, cleanse me and make me brand new. Do Your healing work in me I pray. In Jesus' name, Amen.

Day 101

God Has a Golden Rule

A Truth to Live – God has designed me with the power and ability to shape the way I am treated by others. While others might suggest using techniques of manipulation or bullying, God's way is remarkably simple – treat others the way I desire to be treated. Like a farmer planting seeds, when I "plant" goodness, kindness and mercy into the lives of others, I will "harvest" the same response from them!

Scripture – *"So in everything, do to others what you would have them do to you, for this sums up the Law and the Prophets."* Matthew 7:12

Prayer – Heavenly Father, Your ways are right and just and they create a chain of blessing that passes from one person to another. Help me today to turn away from the idea that I need to manipulate others toward my ends, and instead teach me the power of the golden rule – to do for others what I desire for them to do for me. In Jesus' name, Amen.

Day 102

God's Forgiveness Brings Healing

A Truth to Live – God has created in the heart of every person the perfect recipe of reconciliation and restoration. He knows what I need and has built inside of me the tools to bring harmony and peace with others. FORGIVENESS. When I forgive others it activates something in them to also forgive. And when I extend forgiveness to others God rushes in to forgive me.

Scripture – *"Do not judge, and you will not be judged. Do not condemn, and you will not be condemned. Forgive, and you will be forgiven."* Luke 6:37

Prayer – Forgiving and Merciful Father, teach me today the power that comes in forgiving others first. There are times when I am hurt that my heart wants to demand forgiveness rather than be the one to extend it first. Help me to understand that when I give forgiveness, You rush in and forgive me! Teach me to have a forgiving heart. In Jesus' name, Amen.

Day 103

Repentance Paves the Way for Restoration

A Truth to Live – God has a plan that rebuilds broken relationships and restores the wounds of hurtful words. It starts when I have a heart of grace that asks for forgiveness for wrongs done and then honors others who have a change of heart. When God sees a repentant heart in me He pours out blessing and healing!

Scripture – *The son said, "Father, I have sinned against heaven and against you. I am no longer worthier to be called your son…but the father was filled with compassion, threw his arms around him and kissed him. He said, 'this son of mine was dead and is alive again; he was lost and is found."*
Luke 15:17-24

Prayer – Eternal God, thank You for creating a way for me to restore the broken relationships that have caused pain in my life. I will go and ask forgiveness and seek compassion from those I have offended. Help me to extend the love and grace that You have given me. In Jesus' name, Amen.

Day 104

God Uses Conflicts to Improve My Character

A Truth to Live – God has designed a personal improvement plan for my life. He brings good gifts to me and even uses conflict and difficulty to strengthen and improve my character. When trouble comes, I will turn to God and embrace Him. God will build me into something stronger and better for His name!

Scripture – *"You intended to harm me, but God intended it for good to accomplish what is now being done, the saving of many lives."* Genesis 50:20

Prayer – Heavenly Father, You are trustworthy and know what is good for me. I ask today that You would strengthen my character in difficult times, and deliver me from evil so that the blessings in my life can flow from me to others in need. In Jesus' name, Amen.

Day 105

God Has a Plan that Overcomes Evil

A Truth to Live – God's plan for me includes a prescription for me to thrive in the midst of conflict and to create peaceful relationships in the midst of great difficulty. When I am wronged, our natural inclination is to repay or seek revenge, but it is God's place to pass judgment and it is my place to 'disarm' conflicts by overcoming evil with good.

Scripture – *"Do not be overcome with evil, but overcome evil with good."* Romans 12:17-21

Prayer – Heavenly Father, I will praise You today, because You alone have the strength and wisdom to discern good from evil. You are a righteous judge and will reward us for the good that we do. Help me today to overcome the evil around me with good and to bless others in Your name. In Jesus' name, Amen

Day 106

Choose to Live in Peace

A Truth to Live – God's best for me is a life that is founded on His righteousness and peace. While there are times that confrontation may be necessary, God places a priority on honoring others and creating an environment of peace and harmony in relationships.

Scripture – *"Live in harmony with one another…Do not repay anyone evil with evil. Be careful to do what is right in the eyes of everybody. If it is possible, as far as it depends on you, live at peace with everyone."* Romans 12:16-18

Prayer – Father of Peace, You are my strength and You have the power to heal broken relationships. Grant me today the power to seek Your peace and forgiveness with my peers, family and friends so that they will honor You and live in peace. In Jesus' name, Amen.

Day 107

God is the Sovereign Ruler of the Universe

A Truth to Live – God is an expert in taking things that don't fit, are broken and not even formed and making them into something beautiful. He brought order from chaos and created the heavens and the earth. As the God of order who is in charge of everything, life works best when I follow the structures that He has put in place in the family, the church, the workplace and in the government.

Scripture – *"Everyone must submit himself to the governing authorities, for there is no authority except that which God has established. The authorities that exist have been established by God."* Romans 13:1

Prayer – Eternal Creator, I trust You today. You created the earth and everything in it. You have ordered my days, designed my present and can see my future. Help me to follow the good and righteous plan that You have put before me. In Jesus' name, Amen.

Day 108

God Made the Family

A Truth to Live – God's ideal for the family is one father, one mother and children. His chain of command in Scripture is clear: husband-wife-children. He asks husbands to give their lives for their wives, wives to follow the godly leadership of their husbands and children to honor and obey their parents. Both parents are responsible to train their children to grow in the fear of the Lord and in favor with God and man.

Scripture – *"My son, keep your father's commands and do not forsake your mother's teaching. Bind them upon your heart forever; fasten them around your neck. Husbands love your wives as Christ loved the church, wives submit/follow your husbands as unto the Lord."* Proverbs 6:20-21, Ephesians 5:21-6:4

Prayer – Heavenly Father, teach me today to begin to walk toward You and the path of healing that You have for my family. Help me to live each day faithful to Your Word and to begin to change my conversation and love toward my family so that Your blessings will become my inheritance. In Jesus' name, Amen.

Day 109

God Created Government

A Truth to Live – God's best for me is to live and serve under a government that follows the truths and principles of His Scripture. In this way people are cared for, the poor are given opportunity and the rich become generous with what has been entrusted to them. Living honorable lives within my community will showcase the glory of God even when governments fail to meet God's standards.

Scripture – *"Submit yourselves for the Lord's sake to every authority instituted among men: whether to the king, as the supreme authority, or to governors, who are sent by him to punish those who do wrong and to commend those who do right…show proper respect to everyone: love the brotherhood of believers, fear God, honor the king."* 1 Peter 2:13-17

Prayer – Gracious and Merciful Father, You rule from Your throne in Heaven. Thank You for designing government to punish the wrong and commend those who do right. Help me today to pray for my leaders and to honor You in my words and conduct. In Jesus' name, Amen.

Day 110

God Ordained His Church

A Truth to Live – God cares for my soul, and He created a way for me to be nourished, fed and led in the right direction. First through His Son, and now by the power of His Spirit, God chooses to dwell and make Himself known among those who follow the way, the truth and the life. When I choose to be guided by godly leaders in the church God's protection and provision will become abundant in my life.

Scripture – *"Obey your leaders and submit to their authority. They keep watch over you as men who must give an account. Obey them so that their work will be a joy, not a burden, for that would be of no advantage to you."* Hebrews 13:17

Prayer – Eternal Wise God, thank You for coming and dwelling with us. First through the gift of life in Your Son, Jesus, and now through the power of Your Spirit You grant us life, purpose, direction and care. Help me to enjoy Your abundance by honoring and obeying those who are in spiritual authority in my life. In Jesus' name, Amen.

Day 111

God Anointed Business

A Truth to Live – In the very beginning He gave me dominion over the resources of this earth (Genesis 1:26) and asked me to take responsibility for its care. My work matters to God. He designed me to work with excellence and to be productive for His glory so that everyone could see that I work to please God and not my peers.

Scripture – *"Whatever you do, work at it with all your heart, as working for the Lord and not for men, since you know that you will receive an inheritance from the Lord as a reward. It is the Lord Christ you are serving."* Colossians 3:23-24

Prayer – Heavenly Father, thank You for creating work, the economy and business. You have given us the power to create wealth, and I rejoice today in the pleasure You receive when I do my absolute best. Help me to keep Your perspective on my daily responsibilities so that my inheritance will last! In Jesus' name, Amen.

Day 112

Everyone is Accountable to God

A Truth to Live – There is no escaping it. One day I will stand before God and give an account of every word and deed I have done. The best way to "stay" in a place of blessing is to follow the truth of God's Word with my relationships and my daily conduct. God blesses those who live humbly with others..

Scripture – *"Young men, in the same way be submissive to those who are older. All of you, clothe yourselves with humility toward one another, because God opposes the proud but gives grace to the humble. Humble yourselves, therefore, under God's might hand, that he may lift you up in due time. Cast all your anxiety on Him because He cares for you."*
1 Peter 5:5-7

Prayer – Loving and Eternal Father, thank You for designing me to be interdependent with others. I am grateful for the input of others in my life and am humbled when others ask for my advice. I ask that You teach me to be accountable to You and to others. In Jesus' name, Amen.

Day 113

God Rewards Obedience

A Truth to Live – God is a rewarder of every person who diligently seeks Him (Hebrews 11:6) and has created a system for me to live under the abundance of His blessings. Because He takes a personal interest in how I live, how I treat others and whom I worship, God offers immense rewards when I obey.

Scripture – *"God opposes the proud but gives grace to the humble."* 1 Peter 5:5

Prayer – Heavenly Father, today I am thankful that You are a rewarder of those who diligently seek You. Rather than boast about my small accomplishments I commit to honor You, to give You glory and to exalt Your name today. I choose to be on Your side of history. In Jesus' name, Amen.

Day 114

God Takes the Pressure Off

A Truth to Live – Understanding that God holds the title deed to all of creation helps to alleviate the stress of striving to create something over which I have little if any control. For the Jesus follower, it gets even better – I am doubly cared for. God created me, knows what is best for me, and when I trust in His way to salvation He has permission to guide me through life's ups and downs.

Scripture – *"The earth is the LORD's, and everything in it, the world, and all who live in it; for he founded it upon the seas and established it upon the waters."* Psalms 24:1-2

Prayer – Heavenly Father, You are trustworthy. I know that You created my world and have my best interest in mind. Help me to rest in Your leadership and to honor Your choices in my life. I know that good will come of where I am and what You have me doing. In Jesus' name, Amen.

Day 115

God Holds it All Together for Good

A Truth to Live – God is able. When faced with any trial, pain or difficulty it is comforting to know that God is able – able to redeem, forgive, to sustain, to empower, to love, to overcome, to grant peace and hold it all together. God's capacity to bring good out of where I am helps to release stress and misplaced anxiety or anger. God is good and His plans are always for the better.

Scripture – *"For by him all things were created: things in heaven and on earth, visible and invisible, whether thrones or powers or rulers or authorities; all things were created by him and for him. He is before all things, and in him all things hold together."* Colossians 1:16-17

Prayer – Gracious Father, I turn to You today, because I realize that You are holding it all together - the earth, everything in it, even me and my life's future. Thank You God for being in complete control and for having my best in mind. You are trustworthy. Help me to rest in the comfort of Your eternally good plans. In Jesus' name, Amen.

Day 116

Taking Responsibility Honors God

A Truth to Live – God gives me the opportunity each day to honor Him by taking responsibility for the privileges and opportunities that He has laid before me. Provision, guidance and even the creativity to cultivate friendships and expand my horizons all come from Him. When I use them for His glory and live responsibly God is honored.

Scripture – *"So whether you eat or drink or whatever you do, do it all for the glory of God."* 1 Corinthians 10:31

Prayer – Heavenly Father, You alone are Love and apart from You there is nothing, God. Help me to maintain a gracious perspective that takes responsibility for Your amazing gifts and honors You by my stewardship of Your goodness. In Jesus' name, Amen.

Day 117

Honoring God Reduces Conflict

A Truth to Live – God has created expectations for me. They begin with a recognition that He is in control and grow with the understanding that He has good in store for all of His creation. Honoring others and all of His creation when situations get tense always reduces misunderstanding and conflict.

Scripture – *"Pride only breeds quarrels, but wisdom is found in those who take advice."* Proverbs 13:10

Prayer – Heavenly Father, thank You for helping me to grow through times of pressure and conflict. Today I am choosing not to focus on my "rights" but instead on the beauty that You have created in everyone around me – especially in those with whom I disagree. I know that You value them, even if their choices are not in keeping with Your Word. Help me to be a conduit of Your blessing today. In Jesus' name, Amen.

Day 118

God Doesn't Want Me to Worry

A Truth to Live – God has created a journey for me to follow that is anxiety free. It begins with transferring the ownership of my life to God and then enjoying the overflow of His abundant provision, guidance and eternal peace. God's ways are best, and I can have confidence that when I yield to Him, He will create a better present and future for me.

Scripture – *"Do you not know that your body is a temple of the Holy Spirit, who is in you, whom you have received from God? You are not your own; you were bought at a price. Therefore honor God with your body."* 1 Corinthians 6:19-20

Prayer – Gracious Father, thank You for extending Your eternal love to me through the sacrificial gift of Your Son Jesus. I choose to entrust my present and future to You and ask that You would help me honor You with my mind, my spirit and my body. I know that You have my best interests in mind. In Jesus' name, Amen.

Day 119

God's Ways Create Peace and Rest

A Truth to Live – God has a plan that protects my heart from being hurt when life's interruptions suddenly change my well-intended plans. Since He is in charge of my life, knows the times and places I am to live and has my best interest in mind, I can be thankful that God is looking out for my best – every time!

Scripture – *"Give thanks in all circumstances, for this is God's will for you in Christ Jesus."*
1 Thessalonians 5:18

Prayer – Heavenly Father, thank You for being in charge. I will trust You today and know that You have good things in store for me. Instead of worrying, help me to give thanks for who You are. And when I cannot see Your hand at work, I will thank You for Your abundant blessings and trustworthy character. In Jesus' name, Amen.

Day 120

Following God's Plans Always Brings Hope

A Truth to Live – God knows the best path to take, the right answer to give and the wise decision to make. Even better, He promises to instruct and teach His children in the way they should go. There is no better guide for life than God Himself. He loves me and has only good things in store for me.

Scripture – *"I will instruct you and teach you in the way you should go; I will counsel you and watch over you. Do not be like the horse or the mule, which have no understanding but must be controlled by bit and bridle or they will not come to you. Many are the woes of the wicked, but the LORD's unfailing love surrounds the man who trusts in him. Rejoice in the LORD and be glad, you righteous; sing, all you who are upright in heart!"* Psalms 32:8-11

Prayer – Eternal Loving Father, thank You for the promise of Your leadership and guidance in my life. I admit today that I have a tendency to rely on my own limited abilities. Help me to change and to think first of Your ways, Your paths and to trust in Your unfailing love when I cannot see the way. In Jesus' name, Amen.

Day 121

God's Seal of Salvation Brings Blessing

A Truth to Live – God extends grace to me when I trust in His Son, Jesus, to be my Savior. Rather than basing my present and my future on my daily performance, God instead chooses to give me the gift of His Spirit as a seal, guaranteeing the abundant blessings of His presence now and the eternal inheritance with God in heaven.

Scripture – *"And you also were included in Christ when you heard the word of truth, the gospel of your salvation. Having believed, you were marked in him with a seal, the promised Holy Spirit, who is a deposit guaranteeing our inheritance until the redemption of those who are God's possession--to the praise of his glory."* Ephesians 1:13-14

Prayer – Heavenly Father, thank You for extending Your love and grace to me! Today I receive Your salvation and rest in the presence of Your Spirit guiding and directing my life. Help me to look to You at each moment of my day and to live in a way that gives You glory. In Jesus' name, Amen.

Day 122

God's Spirit Gives Me the Power to Do Right

A Truth to Live – God's has placed His Spirit inside of me so that I have the power to overcome the temptations of this world. His presence dwelling inside of me transforms my temporal desires so that they are God-focused and pleasing to Him. When I live by the Spirit, I will no longer cave into the desires of my sinful nature.

Scripture – *"So I say, live by the Spirit, and you will not gratify the desires of the sinful nature."* Galatians 5:16

Prayer – Gracious Father, thank You for granting me the power to do right. I receive and will follow the promptings of Your Spirit dwelling inside of me today. Help me to put aside my carnal and temporal desires and re-direct my attention to You, to Your good plans for me, and for the privilege of walking with You. In Jesus' name, Amen.

Day 123

God's Ways are Filled with Reward

A Truth to Live – God's Word is filled with promises, with instructions and with principles that guide His creation. His Word is true, it comes true and it stays true every day. When I point my life toward the blessings of His presence, God rewards me with overflowing joy and blessing.

Scripture – *"Do not be deceived: God cannot be mocked. A man reaps what he sows. The one who sows to please his sinful nature, from that nature will reap destruction; the one who sows to please the Spirit, from the Spirit will reap eternal life. Let us not become weary in doing good, for at the proper time we will reap a harvest if we do not give up."* Galatians 6:7-9

Prayer – Eternal Father, help me today to follow Your path. You have created it for my good, and I want to invest in Your ways so that I will reap a harvest of blessing. I choose to invest in Your kingdom, to follow Your ways, and to share Your goodness with others so that they will experience Your abundance. Thank You for generously meeting all my needs and creating in me a heart of generosity. In Jesus' name, Amen.

Day 124

God Wants to Speak

A Truth to Live – The words of God have great power to create, comfort, direct the present and shape the future. The Good News is that God is by nature good and not evil. He wants to bless me, to speak good things into my life and reveal His heart and nature to me.

Scripture – *"The boy Samuel ministered before the LORD under Eli. In those days the word of the LORD was rare; there were not many visions."* 1 Samuel 3:1

Prayer – Heavenly Father, I will still my heart and quiet my mind today so that You can fill it with Your goodness and revelation. I know that You want to reveal Your plans to those who will listen and desire for their path to be straight. Help me to listen and obey. In Jesus' name, Amen.

Day 125

God is a Vision Giving God

A Truth to Live – God wants to be involved in the everyday activities of my life. He has dreams, and goals for me; visions that will help me chart the course of my life. When I choose to spend time with God today away from the noise of life, I will be refreshed!

Scripture – *"So Nathan went back to David and told him everything the LORD had said."* I Chronicles 17:15

Prayer – Heavenly Father, I open my world to You today. Please come and take over every aspect of my life. Show me the way to live wisely, to be filled with joy and to be content with what You have provided. I will rejoice in You. In Jesus' name, Amen.

Day 126

God Creates and Records History

A Truth to Live – History is not a result of random elements in the universe colliding together by accident. Our world is based on the design of a Creator who charts the course of humankind and records its deeds so that I can learn from Him and from others.

Scripture – *"Hezekiah's love for God and the other things he did as king are written in the vision of the prophet Isaiah son of Amoz. This is in the book of the kings of Judah and Israel."* 2 Chronicles 32:32

Prayer – Heavenly Father, I trust You. You were before everything began because You created it, and You are still creating. I trust You today to speak into my life and shape my history for Your glory. In Jesus' name, Amen.

Day 127

God Sets the Course for My Life

A Truth to Live – God desires to be with me, to dwell inside of me and to lead me to good places created with His beauty. When I wait for His presence to guide me, God promises to walk with me each moment of every day.

Scripture – *"The promise is for you and your children and for all who are far off – for all whom the Lord our God will call." Acts 2:39*

Prayer – Heavenly Father, You have promised Your children the gift of Your presence. No longer will I venture out independently with my own ideas. Beginning today, Your Holy Spirit and Your Word will be my compass. I choose to wait for Your presence to lead and guide me. In Jesus' name, Amen.

Day 128

God's Word Brings Blessings

A Truth to Live – If I am in a place of confusion or despair I can take great hope in the reality that God speaks to those who worship Him. He desires to give me strength, courage and endurance, and He honors my love and allegiance to Him.

Scripture – *"You once spoke in a vision to your prophet and said, "I have given help to a warrior. I have selected him from the common people to be king."* Psalms 89:19

Prayer – Gracious Heavenly Father, I know that You want to help me do well in life. You have more wisdom than I can understand, more love than I can grasp and more mercy than I deserve. Help me today to listen to the quiet thunder of Your voice. May it provide direction for today and set the course for my tomorrow. In Jesus' name, Amen.

Day 129

God Uses Others to Reveal His Best for Me

A Truth to Live – God has a plan for my life that is revealed in power through Himself, others and directly to me. Because He knows that directions can be lost, misinterpreted or forgotten He often expresses the roadmap for my journey in the context of relationships with others.

Scripture – "*These visions concerning Judah and Jerusalem came to Isaiah son of Amoz during the reigns of Uzziah, Jotham, Ahaz, and Hezekiah -- all kings of Judah.*" Isaiah 1:1

Prayer – Gracious and Merciful Heavenly Father, thank You for promising to reveal Yourself and Your plans to me. I now understand that the fullest expression of Your revelation comes through the relationships that I have with others who are following You. Help me today to seek their wisdom and counsel and, together, find Your perfect peace. In Jesus' name, Amen.

Day 130

God Always Reveals the Truth

A Truth to Live – There are many voices in my culture shouting out attention-getting falsehoods and manipulating the hearts of the broken. Their lies lead to despair and destruction, but God always reveals a hope that is based on His truth.

Scripture – *"Then the LORD said, "These prophets are telling lies in my name. I did not send them or tell them to speak. I did not give them any messages. They prophesy of visions and revelations they have never seen or heard. They speak foolishness made up in their own lying hearts."* Jeremiah 14:14

Prayer – Heavenly Father, You are the author of truth and in You there are no lies and there are no words that wound or manipulate. Grant me discernment today, that I might be filled with the nourishment of Your Word and grow in You. In Jesus' name, Amen.

Day 131

God's Word Brings Clarity

A Truth to Live – Every good gift that comes from God lines up with the standard, the truth of His Word. Since God can not lie and will not violate what He has decreed, His words are safe, trustworthy and always bring clarity.

Scripture – *" 'This is my warning to my people,' says the LORD Almighty. 'Do not listen to these prophets when they prophesy to you, filling you with futile hopes. They are making up everything they say. They do not speak for the LORD!' "* Jeremiah 23:16

Prayer – Loving and Gracious Father, how grateful I am today that You always bring clarity and purpose to the confusion that swirls around me. Help me today to base what I do and to evaluate what I hear on the never-changing truths of Your Word. They are more valuable than life itself. In Jesus' name, Amen.

Day 132

God Desires to Speak to Those Who Will Listen

A Truth to Live – Each day presents an opportunity to hear from numerous opinions and multiple voices. God places the truth and blessing of His Word into my life when I listen and obey. But when I stop following His commands God withdraws His blessing in hopes that I will return to Him.

Scripture – *"Jerusalem's gates have sunk into the ground. All their locks and bars are destroyed, for he has smashed them. Her kings and princes have been exiled to distant lands; the law is no more. Her prophets receive no more visions from the LORD."* Lamentations 2:9

Prayer – Ever-A-Truth-to-Live God, today I come to You with ears ready to hear. Help my heart to be filled with Your truth and to guide my mind to work and walk according to Your Word. I know that You protect and guide those who are walking in Your path, and I choose to be known as one who will listen and obey. In Jesus' name, Amen.

Day 133

God Rewards the Faithful but Punishes Evil

A Truth to Live – God has established His world to operate on the principles and truths of His Word. When people are faithful to His Word there is an eternal reward that begins to work in their lives. At the same time, wrong doers are responsible for their attitudes and actions and bring God's judgment into their lives.

Scripture – *"And if any merchants should survive, they will never return to their business. For what God has said applies to everyone – it will not be changed! Not one person whose life is twisted by sin will recover."* Ezekiel 7:13

Prayer – God You are Sovereign and the world is under Your control. I ask You to help me live my life according to Your Word and to experience the abundance that comes with obedience. At the same time, grant me the boldness to explain the truth of Your Word and the evil consequences that will come to those who reject Your truth. In Jesus' name, Amen.

Day 134

God Reveals

A Truth to Live – When people live by their own standards, not God's, and follow the craving of their own hearts the results are devastating. In mercy God allows the consequences of evil to become evident in the hope that those who are lost will find their way in Him.

Scripture – *"Trouble after trouble will come. One report will follow another. But they will not be true. The people will try to get visions from the prophets. But there will not be any. The teaching of the law by the priests will be gone. So will advice from the elders. The king will be filled with sadness. The princes will lose all hope. The hands of the people of the land will tremble. I will punish them based on how they have lived. I will judge them by their own standards. Then they will know that I am Lord."* Ezekiel 7:26-27

Prayer – Eternally Wise God, I ask for mercy today. I will turn my thoughts back to You and will share the power of Your truth with others. In mercy forgive us and restore to us the joy of our salvation. Redeem us back from the darkness that surrounds us. In Jesus' name, Amen.

Day 135

Mortal Visions Do Not Last

A Truth to Live – Every day I hear the newly trumpeted claims and promises of hope that come from the mouths and hearts of humankind. Visions and dreams, even leadership direction that comes from the heart of a person may shine brightly for a moment, but in time, they will fade away. Only visions and dreams that come from the heart of God will last.

Scripture – *"Son of man, what is this proverb you have in the land of Israel: 'The days go by and every vision comes to nothing'?"* Ezekiel 12:22

Prayer – Eternal Father, You are the only one who can see. Since You are the beginning and the end, I know Lord that Your vision is clear. Help me today to cling to the truths of Your Word and not the temporary voices that may "seem" right at the moment. I will trust in You. In Jesus' name, Amen.

Day 136

God's Vision is Pure and Eternal

A Truth to Live – Knowing that God's Word never brings doubt, confusion or discouragement the best thing I can do is cling to God and His Word. Because He is truth and He can always be depended on to be good, holy and pure, what God says and what He puts in motion will always come to pass.

Scripture – *"There will no longer be any false visions or flattering fortunetelling to the people. I, the LORD, will speak. Everything that I say will happen without any more delay. I will say something, and it will happen during your lifetime..."* Ezekiel 12:24-25 (GWT)

Prayer – Heavenly Father, today I am choosing to give You the hopes and dreams that I have crafted for myself; plus the visions and plans others have placed over me. I ask instead to be filled to overflowing with the revelation of who You are and the direction that You desire for me to walk. In Jesus' name, Amen.

Day 137

God's Word Always Proves True

A Truth to Live – Many claim to have the 'answer' for my troubles. But following their contrived plans, schemes, and rituals never bring about lasting peace and real solutions to the questions that fill my mind. But God's Word is different. It is powerful and effective.

Scripture – *"Son of man, the people of Israel are saying, 'His visions won't come true for a long, long time.' Therefore, give them this message from the Sovereign LORD: 'No more delay! I will now do everything I have threatened! I, the Sovereign LORD, have spoken!'."* Ezekiel 12:27-28

Prayer – Heavenly Father, today I choose to follow You. Even when those around me are saying that Your words are not real and that You are not faithful, I will cling to You because I know that what You say always proves true. Help me to believe and to stay faithful to Your Word. In Jesus' name, Amen.

Day 138

God's Word Prevails

A Truth to Live – God has an amazing way of clearing the path for truth. The false promises of a quick fix or voices that declare secrets of success do not last. The hope for my future is not a new plan, a new path, or 'revealed' steps. The truth that I need has already been written as time-tested truth in God's Word.

Scripture – *"They were lying prophets who claimed peace would come to Jerusalem when there was no peace. I, the Sovereign LORD, have spoken!"*
Ezekiel 13:16

Prayer – Heavenly Father, thank You for the power of Your Word. It was true. It is true and it will always be true. Forever. Help me to adjust my life to the powerful truth of Your Word and to allow it to guide and shape my heart toward You. In Jesus' name, Amen.

Day 139

God Grants Wisdom, Understanding and Vision

A Truth to Live – God alone is the Creator and has the power to grant me the wisdom that I need today. As I struggle to gain understanding or seek clear vision about the future, I know God is the generator of all things good and will provide for me just what I need.

Scripture – *"God gave these four young men an unusual aptitude for learning the literature and science of the time. And God gave Daniel special ability in understanding the meanings of visions and dreams."* Daniel 1:17

Prayer – Gracious Eternal Father, You are the great giver of life, the creator of the universe and the dispenser of wisdom. I turn to You today confident of Your love and affection toward me. I humbly ask You for wisdom, for understanding and for clarity for the days ahead. In Jesus' name, Amen.

Day 140

God Wants to Speak to Me Today

A Truth to Live – God is the best communicator in the world. His words are clear, true, honest; and they never change. He is dependable and gentle, but also full of justice and mercy. But the best news is that God wants to speak to me again. Today.

Scripture – *"During the third year of King Belshazzar's reign, I, Daniel, saw another vision, following the one that had already appeared to me."* Daniel 8:1

Prayer – Gracious and Merciful Father, I am so grateful that You want to communicate with me and demonstrate to me Your endless love. Today I will focus my day so that my best time is reserved for You. Teach me to slow down enough so that I can listen to Your words. In Jesus' name, Amen.

Day 141

God Gives Glimpses of Heaven

A Truth to Live – When God speaks it is always about His Kingdom, His will and humankind's response to it. Even when angelic messengers of God communicate they speak of God's glory and reveal His plan. The glimpses of heaven given to me from God will always point me back to Him.

Scripture – *"Then I heard two of the holy ones talking to each other. One of them said, "How long will the events of this vision last? How long will the rebellion that causes desecration stop the daily sacrifices? How long will the Temple and heaven's armies be trampled on?"* Daniel 8:13

Prayer – Heavenly Father, I come to You today in prayer knowing that You are the beginning and the end, and that nothing escapes Your notice or takes You by surprise. I want to thank You that Your revealed word, and the messengers You send my way, always point me to back to You and Your purposes. In Jesus' name, Amen.

Day 142

God Wants to Make His Words Clear

A Truth to Live – God knows that He is infinite and that my understanding is limited. In His mercy He has the power to send messengers, spiritual leaders, and peers to assist me in following His vision and becoming like His Son in character. His patience is guided by an over-arching desire He has for me to understand all that He has for me.

Scripture – *"As I, Daniel, was trying to understand the meaning of this vision, someone who looked like a man suddenly stood in front of me. And I heard a human voice calling out from the Ulai River, 'Gabriel, tell this man the meaning of his vision.' As Gabriel approached the place where I was standing, I became so terrified that I fell to the ground. 'Son of man,' he said, 'you must understand that the events you have seen in your vision relate to the time of the end'."* Daniel 8:15-17

Prayer – Heavenly Father, I thank You for Your patience and mercy. Even when confusion surrounds me and keeps me from understanding and following the simplicity of Your Word, You never give up on me. I ask You to help me to learn from You today. In Jesus' name, Amen.

Day 143

God's Words are Timely

A Truth to Live – God knows just what I need for today. And tomorrow. His wisdom will chart the course for my life and guide me each step of the way because He holds the past, the present and the future in His hands. God's words are fulfilled just at the right time.

Scripture – "*This vision about the twenty-three hundred evenings and mornings is true. But none of these things will happen for a long time, so do not tell anyone about them yet.*" Daniel 8:26

Prayer – All Wise and Eternal God, thank You for being my eternal Father. You know just what I need and have promised to lay before me a path that is filled with Your goodness and mercy. Thank You for forgiving my past, teaching me Your ways in the present and promising to guide my future. In Jesus' name, Amen.

Day 144

God Speaks When I Pray

A Truth to Live – Hearing God's voice most often happens when I listen in prayer. So, when I go to God in prayer I: open His Word, meditate on its truths and then ask the Spirit of God to minister to my spirit. I expect God's mercy and love to come in clarity!

Scripture – "*As I was praying, Gabriel, whom I had seen in the earlier vision, came swiftly to me at the time of the evening sacrifice.*" Daniel 9:21

Prayer – Heavenly Father, today I am choosing to take the time to listen to You in prayer. Help me to reflect on the truths of Your Word and to focus my heart on the healing wisdom that You will send to me. Thank You for the many blessings that come from You. In Jesus' name, Amen.

Day 145

God Puts an End to Evil

A Truth to Live – God is Good. Scripture teaches me that every good and perfect gift comes from Him. He is eternally and forever good. Even better, God is more powerful than evil and is at work in my life, in the world and in the future to rid the world once and for all of spiritual bondage and darkness. I trust Him for good.

Scripture – *"A period of seventy sets of seven has been decreed for your people and your holy city to put down rebellion, to bring an end to sin, to atone for guilt, to bring in everlasting righteousness, to confirm the prophetic vision, and to anoint the Most Holy Place."* Daniel 9:24

Prayer – Good and Merciful God, I know that now, and at the end of time, You are about destroying the work of evil. Help me today to depend on You and to watch for Your hand to be at work in my life every step of the way. In Jesus' name, Amen.

Day 146

God Knows the Future

A Truth to Live – God created everything and that includes the future. Since He charts the course of man's steps and has given every person a free will to choose righteousness or evil, the consequences and future of humankind have been set. The most important decision I can make today is to be on His side.

Scripture – "*Now I am here to explain what will happen to your people in the future, for this vision concerns a time yet to come.*" Daniel 10:14

Prayer – God, I am grateful today that You hold the future in Your hands. You are trustworthy and filled with mercy for those who turn toward You. Today I choose again to call upon You for salvation and the forgiveness of sins. Redeem me through the precious sacrifice of Your Son who died for me. In Jesus' name, Amen.

Day 147

God is in Charge

A Truth to Live – When the END comes, God will still be in charge. Many people believe that government leaders, or economic forces shape the future, but they are misled. God is firmly in charge of the world He created, and when people rise against His ways, they will never prevail.

Scripture – *"At that time there will be a general uprising against the king of the south. Lawless ones among your own people will join them in order to fulfill the vision, but they will not succeed."* Daniel 11:14

Prayer – Eternal God, Your strength will never weaken. Today I turn to You to help me cling to You and not to the voices or forces of this world. I ask for Your direction, guidance and deliverance from all evil as I put my complete trust in You. In Jesus' name, Amen.

Day 148

God Teaches Through His Word

A Truth to Live – God's Word is truth to live by. It is like a lamp to our feet, a light to our path. God's purposes for my life are revealed in His promises and are confirmed by God's desire to see them fulfilled in my life. Every day God has already chosen wisdom for me to find in His Word.

Scripture – *"I sent my prophets to warn you with many visions and parables."* Hosea 12:10

Prayer – Heavenly Father, today I commit to study and apply the truths of Your holy Word. I will consume them like the best food. Help me God to discern and filter the voices that surround me by the time-tested truths of Your Word. I will look to You and to the truth of Your Word to be the guide for my words, my actions and the thoughts of my heart. In Jesus' name, Amen.

Day 149

God Speaks Through His Spirit

A Truth to Live – Just as Jesus announced that the "Spirit of the Lord" was upon Him to announce the Good News so today many claim to have special words or insight from the Lord. I can know if their words are true with a simple test. Does the message that I hear today line up with the life and character of Jesus and His Eternal Word? If so, it will draw me closer to God!

Scripture – *"This is the vision that the Sovereign LORD revealed to Obadiah concerning the land of Edom. We have heard a message from the LORD that an ambassador was sent to the nations to say, 'Get ready, everyone! Let's assemble our armies and attack Edom!'"* Obadiah 1:1

Prayer – Heavenly Father, in You, and You alone, can I find truth and direction for my life. Help me today to measure all that I hear by the truth of who You are and the power of Your Word. Change me to be conformed closer to the image of Your Son so that I can make You known in the earth. In Jesus' name, Amen.

Day 150

God Always Speaks the Truth

A Truth to Live – What happens to people who speak falsehoods in order to make themselves larger than life? God shuts them off. Fortunately God's way is consistently evident. It always involves exalting God and humbling myself by confessing wrongdoing, receiving forgiveness and sharing God's great love with others.

Scripture – *"Now the night will close around you, cutting off all your visions. Darkness will cover you, making it impossible for you to predict the future. The sun will set for you prophets, and your day will come to an end."* Micah 3:6

Prayer – Eternal Father of Light and Truth, I need Your help today to keep me from listening to and following those who want to promote themselves instead of You. Help me to humble myself toward You, to be honest about my shortcomings and openly receive Your love. In Jesus' name, Amen.

Day 151

God Has a Message for Me

A Truth to Live – God's love for me compels Him to share His best with me. He knows that left on my own mistakes will be made and that I will be lost. I can rest in the truth that God has a revelation of His love and His Kingdom for me today. I will search for it and find Him!

Scripture – *"This message concerning Nineveh came as a vision to Nahum, who lived in Elkosh."*
Nahum 1:1

Prayer – Eternal God, You are the revealer of all truth and wisdom. I know that in times past You have spoken clearly to people providing for them a path to life and eternity with You. You are still speaking through Your Word and through those who serve You. I will listen today for your revelation and direction. In Jesus' name, Amen.

Day 152

God Speaks So That I Can Understand

A Truth to Live – God is a revealing, communicating God. He wants me to know Him, to understand His ways and to follow Him. He does not hide His truth or make Himself difficult to find. When the Good News comes to me, I will share it completely, simply and frequently with others. In that God is pleased.

Scripture – *"Then the LORD said to me, 'Write my answer in large, clear letters on a tablet, so that a runner can read it and tell everyone else'."* Habakkuk 2:2

Prayer – Heavenly Father, I need to hear from You today. In fact I am desperate to know You and Your ways. Help me to spend my best time listening, reading and meditating on Your truth so that I can effectively and simply share it with others. In Jesus' name, Amen.

Day 153

God's Word is Always On Time

A Truth to Live – God knows the past, what is happening right now and what is to be. I can trust that His words for me will come to pass at just the right time. I will be sure that what I have heard is true to His Word and not grow weary or give up hope. God is never late and His words will come true!

Scripture – *"But these things I plan won't happen right away. Slowly, steadily, surely, the time approaches when the vision will be fulfilled. If it seems slow, wait patiently, for it will surely take place. It will not be delayed."* Habakkuk 2:3

Prayer – Heavenly Father, I thank You for speaking truth and direction into my life through the power of Your Word and the gentle guidance of those who follow You. Teach me to be patient today, unwavering in courage and filled with strength while I wait in hope for Your truth to be revealed. In Jesus' name, Amen.

Day 154

God Makes His Way Known

A Truth to Live – God's greatest desire is for me to walk in wholeness, to live a full life, and to spend eternity with Him. But knowing that I could never find this joy on my own, God sent His only Son to earth. He commissioned Him to live and walk among men, that through Him I might have eternal life here and the life to come.

Scripture – *"The word became flesh and made His dwelling among us. We have seen His glory, the glory of the One and Only, who came from the Father, full of grace and truth."* John 1:14

Prayer – Heavenly Father, thank You for making Your way known to me. You are Love and I receive all that You have for me today. I will follow the teaching and the steps of Your Son, Jesus, because I know that He alone is the way, the truth and the life. In Jesus' name, Amen.

Day 155

God-Centered Conversation Brings Life to Me and to Those Around Me

A Truth to Live – Looking for life in a dark situation? The way out may be simpler than I think! Instead of following the crowd – finding fault, yielding to negative thoughts and conversation or discouragement – I will choose to follow the path of Proverbs 10:11.

I will study God's Word and allow God's Word to overflow in my heart; then I can position my response to be seasoned with His wisdom, tenderness and mercy. I will become a "fountain of life" and a friend to those in need.

Scripture – *"The mouth of the righteous is a fountain of life, but violence overwhelms the mouth of the wicked."* Proverbs 10:11

Prayer – Dear Lord, today I pray that Your Word would breathe through me throughout the day. When faced with difficult circumstances or unpleasant conversations I ask that You would allow me to be a "fountain of life," focusing on the solutions and comfort that Your Word brings. In Jesus' name, Amen.

Day 156

Abundant Life Springs From a Protected Heart and a Pure Mouth

A Truth to Live – What does wisdom suggest my top priority should be? It is to guard my heart. When coarse conversation, negative thoughts or desiring eyes distract me from following Jesus, my heart becomes filled with unhealthy and non-producing fuel for life. How can I tell if I am putting the right fuel into my mind and spirit? Jesus described it simply when He said, *"Out of the overflow of the heart, the mouth speaks."* (Matthew 12:34)

The best way to find abundant life is to guard my heart from evil and keep my conversation pure, wholesome and uplifting.

Scripture – *"Above all else, guard your heart, for it is the wellspring of life. Put away perversity from your mouth; keep corrupt talk from your lips."*
Proverbs 4:23-24

Prayer – Dear Lord, I make a commitment to guard my heart from clinging to a painful past and focus instead on the goodness of Your character I am discovering in Your Word. I choose to stop using coarse, critical or sarcastic language that does not edify You, others or me. By choosing to live out Your Word in my daily conversation I believe that I will begin to see my own heart overflow with goodness. In Jesus' name, Amen.

Day 157

God's Word Provides Focus and Instruction to My Life

A Truth to Live – Surviving the twists and turns of life without God's Word is as difficult as driving without directions! It is easy to get lost, drive in circles, or even worse, reach a dead end.

How fortunate I am to have been given a roadmap that provides practical instruction and wisdom for every circumstance that may come my way. I can count on God's Word to be my true source of wisdom and direction.

This treasured roadmap contains divine inspiration and a way through every difficulty. I will focus on learning God's truth by memorizing His Word. I choose to allow His Word to be "life" to me!

Scripture – *"Hold on to instruction, do not let it go; guard it well, for it is your life."* Proverbs 4:13

Prayer – Dear Lord, today I choose to allow Your Word to be my instruction. I will use it like a roadmap, to guide me through the complexities of my day and to illuminate my way in every conversation. You alone God, hold the truth. I ask You to help me focus on Your instruction and to discover Your "life" in me. In Jesus' name, Amen.

Day 158

Applying the Word of God to My Plans Brings His Purposes Into Reality

A Truth to Live – The 18th century Scottish Poet, Robert Burns said, "the best laid plans of mice and men often go awry." Why is this so? It is simply because I have limited resources, limited views and a limited capacity. My plans often just don't work out.

But *"with God all things are possible."* (Luke 1:37) When I choose to apply God's Word to my ideals something amazing happens. My weak attempts to find solutions become infused with God's wisdom and revelation. His Word prevails.

Scripture – *"Many are the plans in a man's heart, but it is the Lord's purpose that prevails."* Proverbs 19:21

Prayer – Heavenly Father, Your Word is true and filled with wisdom. I pray today that the feebleness of my own plans would be strengthened, shaped and guided by the power of Your Word. May Your good and abundant purposes begin to work in my life. In Jesus' name, Amen.

Day 159

God's Word is a Shield of Protection

A Truth to Live – Sometimes my words lead me to a place in conversation that I regret. I can be thankful that I have access to God's Word – it is flawless and acts as a shield of protection.

I take refuge in God's Word when His truth is digested in my heart and naturally begins to shape my words. Gentle words replace harsh responses. Kind encouragements are substituted for rash criticisms. Loving support begins to overpower defensiveness. The results? God's Word protects me from the potential pain and discouragement of words gone awry.

Scripture – *"Every word of God is flawless; He is a shield to those who take refuge in Him."* Proverbs 30:5

Prayer – Dear Lord, today I choose to allow Your Word to become my shield and protection. Even before responding to others, I will take the time to seek Your Word so that my replies will be hidden in Your wisdom. In Jesus' name, Amen.

Day 160

Godly Character and Righteous Conversation Lead to Godly Children

A Truth to Live – What do I have that is worthy to pass along to the next generation? Talent? Genius? Education? Heritage? While all these are good traits, none of them are the foundation stones of a fruitful life. More than anything else those watching and emulating my life are looking for a confident strength that comes from a relationship with Jesus Christ.

Having a righteous character requires having the right unselfish motives to do the right things all the time – even when no one else is looking. To everyone who lives a righteous life, God promises to bless their children.

Scripture – *"The righteous man leads a blameless life; blessed are his children after him."* Proverbs 20:7

Prayer – Dear Heavenly Father, today I surrender to You my internal motives. These deep desires drive my actions, thoughts and my future. I ask You to cleanse my heart so that righteousness has a space to grow my character and shape my conversation. In Jesus' name, Amen.

Day 161

My Mind and Spirit are Fed by the Words I Speak

A Truth to Live – My words have power! Whether they are filled with encouragement and praise or criticism and ridicule, my words become the diet of my own emotional well-being. Just as my body is fueled by the food I digest so my heart and mind are filled by the words that I speak.

When I speak words of life from God's Word I actually feed myself with wisdom, truth and righteousness! The reverse is also true. When I fill my mouth with crass humor, vulgarity or empty talk God's Word is diminished in my heart and mind. What's the answer? Speak and memorize the Word!

Scripture – *"From the fruit of his mouth a man's stomach is filled; with the harvest from his lips he is satisfied."* Proverbs 18:20

Prayer – Dear Lord, I realize that my words need to reflect Your Word more each day. Today, I commit to increase my reading of Your Word and then to memorize and digest it so that my heart and mind are fed with Your eternal truth, mercy and wisdom. In Jesus' name, Amen.

Day 162

God is the Revealer of Wisdom

A Truth to Live – Every year thousands of new books are published, seminars are given and infomercials are produced offering "insight" into the world of relationships, finances, career advancement and a host of other topics. But there is only one true source for wisdom – GOD. Since God designed the Word to be filled with wisdom, knowledge, understanding and common sense, the BEST decision I can make on a daily basis is to read, study and apply the truths found in His Word.

Scripture – *"For the Lord gives wisdom, and from His mouth come knowledge and understanding."* Proverbs 2:6

Prayer – Dear Lord, You have already created THE source for revelation, wisdom and knowledge! Your Word is A Truth to Live, and it is filled the answers for every issue or difficulty I could possibly face. Today I ask that You would help me to focus my learning on the "Truth to Live" of Your Word and to cease from depending solely on man's best advice. I ask that You help me to adjust my conversations so that they are no longer filled with the meager opinions of man, but that they overflow with Your eternal wisdom. In Jesus' name. Amen.

Day 163

Applying God's Word Brings Wisdom and Discernment

A Truth to Live – Keeping a pure mind and a righteous heart are the beginning steps required to cultivate wise conversations. In fact, when I make the effort to digest the never-changing truth of God's Word I am often "surprised" at the wise counsel that flows from my own lips. In Isaiah 55:11 the Lord declares that "*the word that goes out from My mouth; will not return to Me empty.*" Wisdom flows from the mouth of the righteous because God Himself is the guarantee of His Word.

Scripture – *"The mouth of the righteous brings forth wisdom, but a perverse tongue will be cut out."* Proverbs 10:31

Prayer – Dear Heavenly Father, You are the only true and wise One. I commit today to take the first steps toward wisdom – maintaining a pure mind and righteous heart. I will be sure to not carelessly comment on the issues of the day without first seeking Your wisdom. I ask that You fill my mouth with answers that display Your wisdom. In Jesus' name, Amen.

Day 164

Godly Wisdom Provides Timely Solutions

A Truth to Live – There is tremendous power in the spoken word. My conversations can showcase my knowledge or bring embarrassment because of hidden ignorance. The Word of God is a trusted, reliable source of eternal yet practical truth. When I allow my conversations to be filtered through the principles of His Word, others will hear wisdom flowing from my lips and recognize an internal calmness that surpasses the crisis of the moment.

Scripture – *"Even a fool is thought wise if he keeps silent, and a man of understanding is even tempered."* Proverbs 17:28

Prayer – Dear Lord, You alone are the only wise God. Today I commit to open Your Word and learn. I will digest Your truth so that the words of my mouth reveal Your wisdom and not my own limited understanding. In Jesus' name, Amen.

Day 165

God's Purposes Prevail When I Yield to His Authority

A Truth to Live – How do my finite and flawed plans compare with the eternally correct and wise plans of God? He sees the whole of everything I see in part. He is the source and creator of all resources; I am dependent on His provision. He is both the beginning and the end; my life is but a breath. It makes sense then to submit my best thoughts, ideas and plans to the One who created the heavens and earth. Since His plans will prevail in the end, I should start with seeking Him for wisdom and revelation for my daily direction.

Scripture – *"Many are the plans in a man's heart, but it is the Lord's purpose that prevails."* Proverbs 19:21

Prayer – Dear Lord, You are Wise and Your ways are higher than ours. We see in part, You see the whole. Help me today to transfer the preferences of my heart to Your purposes and plans. I trust You to bring comfort and direction to my life so my days will find peace and order. In Jesus' name, Amen.

Day 166

Godly Wisdom Provides the Righteous the Power to Create Lasting Wealth

A Truth to Live – Applying the wise principles of God's Word in my life and conversation shifts both my present and my future towards my destiny. The talents, abilities, skills, life lessons and my material goods are all gifts from God. It is His intention to bless me with these gifts so that, through the power of His Word, I can extend His blessings to multiple generations. When I apply the wisdom of His Word to my daily conversation, it shapes my habits and decisions into legacy-leaving deposits for generations to come!

Scripture – *"A good man leaves an inheritance for his children's children, but a sinner's wealth is stored up for the righteous."* Proverbs 13:22

Prayer – Dear Lord, I choose today to allow Your wisdom to be the dominant force in my decision making and conversation with others. Rather than find confidence in my own experience, I will entrust my future and the future of those I love to Your loving hand. I ask for Your guidance to discover Your principles of wisdom so that I may begin to live out the truth of Your legacy-leaving Word. In Jesus' name, Amen.

Day 167

Whole-hearted Trust in God Results in an Abundant Life

A Truth to Live – Growing strong in God is about "yielding" and total "surrender" more than it is about acquiring knowledge and understanding. Proverbs instructs me to not find confidence in my own intellect or in my ability to problem-solve, but rather to grow in giving Him total trust and eternal credit.

God desires to invest the wisdom of His Word in those who will appreciate it. When facing any difficulty the instruction is clear: I will first trust Him and then give credit for the solution to God alone. He then will take over the process and make all things that appear crooked and confused straight and simple!

Scripture – *"Trust in the Lord with all your heart and lean not on your own understanding; in all your ways acknowledge Him and He will make your paths straight."* Proverbs 3:5-6

Prayer – Dear Father, living in total trust and giving away temporary credit are things that I find difficult to do. Today I choose a path of trusting You, acknowledging You as the Source of my needs, and waiting on You to show the path I will walk. Teach me to follow this principle so that confusion gives way to clarity and the complexities of life make room for Your clear and direct paths of abundance. In Jesus' name, Amen.

Day 168

God Finds Pleasure in Those Who Prioritize Truth in Conversation

A Truth to Live – In today's "politically correct" world, where conversations are muted by public opinion and people hesitate to speak clearly, God openly declares He "delights" in truthful conversation. I feel the insincerity and shallowness that comes with carefully constructed half-truths and appreciate the kind and honest words of a friend.

How much more then must my Heavenly Father enjoy honest conversation that stretches up to Him in praise and extends, based on the truth of His Word, from one person to another.

Scripture –"*The Lord detests lying lips, but He delights in men who are truthful.*" Proverbs 12:22

Prayer – Dear Lord, all around me people are focused on "sounding" right in their words. Help me instead Lord, to be truthful and say what is "right." I pledge to find ways to be kind and merciful with others but to not deny the truth. In this I know You will be pleased. In Jesus' name. Amen.

Day 169

Godly Conversation Brings Peace to Every Relationship

A Truth to Live – I have the power to shift conversations toward godly values. Regardless of another person's comments made to me, God's Word is clear – my answers can turn away wrath or crank up the anger! The old adage "it takes two to tango" is true. If I choose not to fuel the heat of a conversation, but rather temper it with gentle answers, God's Word will go into effect and His peace will bring transformation – right before my eyes!

Scripture – *"A gentle answer turns away wrath, but a harsh word stirs up anger."* Proverbs 15:1

Prayer – Dear Lord, I believe Your Word! I choose today to see Your hand at work in my conversations – even the difficult ones. Help me to realize that my words can shape the destiny of a conversation. Fill me with the wisdom of Your Word so that I can respond with gentleness and not with wrath! In Jesus' name, Amen.

Day 170

My Conversations Have the Power to Heal or Crush the Spirit of Others

A Truth to Live – Conversations that are uplifting, encouraging and honest bring life to those around me. At the same time, negative, critical, cynical or sarcastic conversations, even if they are humorous for the moment, do not bring healing and hope. In fact they create a reputation that others will drift away from while damaging the emotions of those around me. Over time, healing conversation creates friends while deceitfulness brings isolation and loneliness. I can choose!

Scripture – *"The tongue that brings healing is a tree of life, but a deceitful tongue crushes the spirit."* Proverbs 15:4

Prayer – Dear Lord, I ask that You would give me the courage to begin to take control of my conversations. I recognize that my own words can bring life to others or crush their spirits. Today I choose to focus on the power of Your Word and bring healing to those around me by using uplifting, encouraging and godly conversation. In Jesus' name, Amen.

Day 171

Wisdom Nourishes My Soul and Provides Lasting Hope

A Truth to Live – There is a confident assurance that comes from the wisdom of God's Word. Even in the midst of difficult circumstances I can find peace and rest as I depend on God's Word to work on my behalf. Wisdom is "sweet" to my soul, in that Godly wisdom can provide solutions and direction to my life even if others are trapped in a sea of confusion.

God's Word is not only my rescue from difficulty; it is a *"lamp to my feet and a light to my path."* The future is bright for those who trust in God's Word.

Scripture – "*Know that wisdom is sweet to your soul; if you find it there is a future hope for you, and your hope will not be cut off.*" Proverbs 24:14

Prayer – Dear Heavenly Father, today I will seek wisdom in Your Word. You have placed before me an opportunity to walk out my life with You and be filled with hope. I choose You and Your Word, rather than my own attempts at finding "solutions." Beginning today, I confidently place my future in Your hands and ask that You guide my conversation to reflect the truth of Your Word. In Jesus' name, Amen.

Day 172

Kind Words Encourage Even the Heavy Hearted

A Truth to Live – I often have "unknowingly" over-scheduled and over-burdened my daily routine with the obligations of work, social commitments, and other activities. The result of this "busy" life is often a sense that, rather than managing my own activities, I allow my schedule to control me.

I will first seek the spread of His Kingdom (Matthew 6:33). Second, when I speak God's Word over my own situation and operate conversationally with kindness toward others, God begins to work on my behalf so that His priorities help shape my daily routine, and His mercy extends through my conversations to the hectic lifestyle of those around me. It brings cheer both to me and to those around me!

Scripture – *"An anxious heart weighs a man down, but a kind word cheers him up."* Proverbs 12:25

Prayer – Dear Lord, today I choose to not allow my own "busyness" to keep me from being kind to others. Help me not to be inwardly focused, but to choose Your Kingdom and Your ways. Grant me the opportunity to bring joy and happiness to those around me by replacing my complaints with words that are kind, loving and considerate toward others. In Jesus' name, Amen.

Day 173

A Joy-Filled Heart Brings Health

A Truth to Live – I can make the choice today to have a cheerful heart. It is an amazing power granted to me by our Creator. I can choose to look at my circumstances and be affected by them, or I can choose to have the Word of God impact my circumstances. A heart that is crushed can siphon every bit of life away, but a cheerful disposition restores like a good medicine.

Scripture – *"A cheerful heart is good medicine, but a crushed spirit dries up the bones."* Proverbs 17:22

Prayer – Dear Heavenly Father, today I choose to be cheerful and to look at the blessings You have given me! I will not be brought down by my temporary circumstances any longer; I will choose to rejoice in Your goodness working in my life. Help me to be consistently cheerful in my outlook. In Jesus' name. Amen.

Day 174

Words of Integrity and Trust Create Opportunity for Personal Influence

A Truth to Live – Sometimes I spend enormous amounts of energy and resources "positioning" myself for a promotion and for a better opportunity or to gain power in relationships. However, God's Word offers a clear and never-failing alternative to the work of self-promotion.

God searches throughout the whole earth looking for people who can be trusted with the wisdom of His Word. He promises to open doors for those whose hearts are pure and whose actions are filled with integrity.

Scripture – "*He who loves a pure heart and whose speech is gracious will have the king for his friend.*" Proverbs 22:11

Prayer – Dear Lord, You are eternally wise and promise to provide a future for me that is filled with Your goodness. Teach me to put my hope in You and to focus my heart, not on self-promotion, but rather on staying pure in heart and using words that are gracious and honor others. Then I can trust Your Word to work in me and on my behalf. In Jesus' name, Amen

Day 175

My Words Shape My Destiny

A Truth to Live – Most people prioritize their hard work thinking that it is THE factor that propels them beyond their peers. They expect "effort" to be the dominating influence at work, school and in the neighborhood.

While there is no doubt that work and effort play an important role, God's Word here makes it clear that my words can shape and prosper my future. When I concentrate on creating conversations that respect others and honor God's Word, God promises that good things will come my way.

Scripture – "*From the fruit of his lips a man is filled with good things, as surely as the work of his hands rewards him.*" Proverbs 12:14

Prayer – Dear Heavenly Father, I recognize that there is power in godly conversation. I admit to You that I have, at times, focused more on "effort" and diligence than I have on carefully choosing my words. I am asking for Your wisdom to grant me the courage to increase the focus of my conversation with others so that the "fruit" of my lips will breathe life into the rest of my day. In Jesus' name, Amen.

Day 176

God's Word is the Pathway to Revelation

A Truth to Live – Directionless. Aimless. Pointless. These words describe the person whose life is absent a divine destiny. In reality God's Word provides the revelation I need to focus my life to live above the monotony of sameness and the dullness of a meaningless routine.

I need revelation that speaks of purpose, destiny and future. Where can I find this? The Word teaches me that the "law" – God's covenant – is my guarantee of revelation and blessing.

Scripture – "*Where there is no revelation, the people cast off restraint; but blessed is he who keeps the law.*" Proverbs 29:18

Prayer: Dear Lord, forgive me for being easily distracted by the meaningless data that swarms around my everyday life. Today I seek the revelation available through Your Word and ask You to grant me increased clarity for my divine destiny. You will make known to me the path of life. In Jesus' name, Amen.

Day 177

Wisdom From God's Word Brings Abundance

A Truth to Live – Measuring my life by the truth of God's Word is the best life decision I can make. The Word will teach me who God is, who I am and how I should relate to the Creator. The result? Humility in life and respect for God will bring abundance to every aspect of my life.

Scripture – *"Humility and the fear of the Lord bring wealth and honor and life."* Proverbs 22:4

Prayer – Dear Lord, I need the clarity of focus and purpose that Your Word brings. Today, I commit to base my life on Your Word, and I trust You to work in me to bring abundance to every aspect of my life. In Jesus' name, Amen.

Day 178

God's Word Brings Discernment and Opportunities to Learn

A Truth to Live – While the foolish make hasty and costly decisions, those who apply God's Word to their lives find wisdom even in complex situations. Those who seek the fullness of who God has intended them to be integrate the truth of God's Word and gain wisdom for their heart's desires.

Scripture – *"The wise in heart are called discerning, and pleasant words promote instruction."*
Proverbs 16:21

Prayer – Dear Lord, I desire for my life to be rooted in Your wisdom so that I can navigate each circumstance that comes my way. I know that left to my own understanding I will continue to repeat my mistakes. Teach me, Lord, to apply Your Word so that I may learn from each situation and grow in godly discernment. In Jesus' name, Amen.

Day 179

Diligence Leads to Reward

A Truth to Live – God has placed deep down inside of every person godly desires for provision, healthy relationships, and most importantly, a God connection. At the same time there are other desires that compete for my attention – these are called the desires of the flesh, the desires of the eyes and the desire for control/power (1 John 2:16).

I have been given an opportunity to match my desire with diligent effort. This requires hard work, consistency, focus and the choice to direct my desire and diligence toward godliness.

Scripture – *"The sluggard craves and gets nothing, but the desires of the diligent are fully satisfied."* Proverbs 13:4

Prayer – Dear Lord, today I make the choice to focus my attention on the godly desires of provision, healthy relationships, and my connection with You. I know that these are good choices. I commit to be diligent toward the things You have decided are best for me. In Jesus' name, Amen

Day 180

Answered Prayers Breathe Life

A Truth to Live – There are times when I have patiently waited for something important or an ideal for which I believe strongly to come to fruition. When these dreams do not become a reality frustration and disappointment often set in. Since God is watching over His Word to see it performed (Jeremiah 1:12), I can choose instead to see my prayers answered when I put the power and truth of His Word to work in my lives.

Scripture – *"Hope deferred makes the heart sick, but a longing fulfilled is a tree of life."* Proverbs 13:12

Prayer – Dear Heavenly Father, too many times I have seen my dreams and longings fade into the distant past and not become a reality. Today I ask You to help me begin something new. I will seek to apply Your Word to my life and then watch it breathe life into my daily routine. In Jesus' name, Amen.

Day 181

Generosity Refreshes the Soul

A Truth to Live – The world around me creates celebrities of people who lavishly spend. God's Word, however, promises to honor those who lavishly give. Generosity is the key to a peaceful and refreshed heart because it grants me the opportunity to extend my life to others through the positive influence of giving.

Scripture – *A generous man will prosper: he who refreshes others will himself be refreshed."*
Proverbs 11:25

Prayer – Dear Lord, today I ask You to grant me the opportunity to give – of my time, talents and treasure. Help me to focus, not on what I can take or keep, but rather on what I can invest in others. Giving back will open my eyes to see Your world more clearly and it will refresh my soul. In Jesus' name, Amen.

Day 182

Righteousness Elevates

A Truth to Live – Ever wonder what brings strife and causes separation between people, families, clans and nations? It is not military might or even political strength. God's Word makes it very clear – righteousness exalts a nation and sin is a disgrace to any people. This applies to me as well. God will exalt those who righteously live by the truth of His Word.

Scripture – "*Righteousness exalts a nation, but sin is a disgrace to any people.*" Proverbs 14:34

Prayer – Dear Lord, I ask You today for a brand new start. Help me to separate myself from the selfish behavior of the past and focus on living a righteous and pure life. I am confident that if I will do my part in obedience to You, You will do more than Your share to provide for my every need. In Jesus' name, Amen.

Day 183

My Words Can Please God

A Truth to Live – I have the potential today of bringing joy to the heart of God. The Psalm says that the words of my mouth can be pleasing to God. What an incredible opportunity; I can please God by the words I choose.

Scripture – *"May the words of my mouth and the meditation of my heart be pleasing in Your sight, O Lord, my Rock and my Redeemer."* Psalms 19:14

Prayer – Dear Lord, I ask for the strength today to change my vocabulary so that it pleases You. You have done so much for me, and I want to please Your heart with godly conversation. In Jesus' name, Amen.

Day 184

My Heart Can Please God

A Truth to Live – My emotions and my will can bring joy to the heart of God? He delights in righteous and humble attitudes that refresh others and honor Him. Even in the midst of difficult circumstances and trials I have the power to choose to respond in a way that pleases God.

Scripture – *"May the words of my mouth and the meditation of my heart be pleasing in Your sight, O Lord, my Rock and my Redeemer."* Psalms 19:14

Prayer – Dear Lord, I ask for Your help today. I want to be an example of the joy that humility and selflessness brings to Your heart. For too long I have focused on my own well-being and never considered the reality that I could please You with my heart attitudes. Help me to make a difference for You! In Jesus' name, Amen.

Day 185

Strength for Today

A Truth to Live – God promises me abundant life and contentment in each circumstance if I will do just two things each day – love Him with everything I have; and, care for and love those around me just like I care for myself.

Scripture – *"Love the Lord your God with all your heart and with all your soul and with all your mind."* Matthew 22:37-40

Prayer – Dear Father, I know that You have promised abundant life for me. But I have to admit I choose sometimes to create my own way instead of relying on You to be my source. Help me to depend on You and to love You with every part of my being. In Jesus' name, Amen.

Day 186

Found

A Truth to Live – God knows how easy it is for me to lose my way, or to get sidetracked from the path with "good-intentions." He loves me so much He created a clear path for me to find my way back to Him.

Scripture –"*If we confess our sins, he is faithful and just and will forgive us our sins and purify us from all unrighteousness."* I John 1:9

Prayer – God, You are my Guide, the perfect One to keep me from going astray. Help me to remember that I can find my way back to You through the simple act of admitting my shortcomings and sins. I receive Your forgiveness today. In Jesus' name, Amen.

Day 187

Pleasing You

A Truth to Live – God made me for a purpose. He has a destiny planned out for me and wants me to know and experience all of His goodness. The journey to my peace and destiny begins with a whole-hearted commitment to please Him with all that I am and all that I do.

Scripture – *"In view of God's mercy, offer your bodies as a living sacrifice, holy and pleasing to God as a spiritual act of worship."* Romans 12:1

Prayer – God, today I choose to set aside all of my own desires and dreams. Help me to focus on pleasing You with all that I do and say knowing that You will be honored and I will be protected and strengthened by Your love. In Jesus' name, Amen.

Day 188

The Right Steps to Take

A Truth to Live – God has already published a journey map for my life. Like any treasure worth pursuing His plans require sacrifice and commitment – but it is completely worth the effort.

Scripture – *"Don't be conformed any longer to the pattern of the world, but be transformed by the renewing of your mind."* Romans 12:1-2

Prayer – Heavenly Father, fill me with the power and truth of Your Word. I need to be reminded of my commitment to walk straight and not wonder off in the patterns of the world. Help me to focus my words and actions on Your ways. In Jesus' name, Amen.

Day 189

Follow Hard

A Truth to Live – God has created a path so that I can follow after Him. It is a well-worn path others have travelled, but it is contrary to my human nature. It is about becoming less so that He can become more in me and through me.

Scripture – *"If anyone would come after me, he must deny himself, pick up his cross and follow me."* Matthew 16:24

Prayer – Heavenly Father, today I make the choice to follow hard after You. I will no longer passively include You in my agenda. Instead, I pray that You will help me focus on Your agenda and Your purpose for me. I will deny my own wants and desires so that I can see You clearly. In Jesus' name, Amen.

Day 190

Hide it Well

A Truth to Live – God has already created a way for me to succeed in the battle against evil. Since He knows that the battle rages in my mind and heart, God prepared His Word to be the fuel that keeps me going in the right direction.

Scripture – We will *"seek you with all our hearts; do not let us stray from your commands. We have hidden your word in our hearts so that we might not sin against you."* Psalms 119:9-11

Prayer – Heavenly Father, thank You for Your Word. It is more precious than gold and keeps me from evil. Help me to read, to think about and to meditate on its truth today so that my thoughts will not stray from the good that You have for me. In Jesus' name, Amen.

Day 191

Down is the New Up

A Truth to Live – God chose a path for me that is good. It is not the well-worn, but wearying journey of self-promotion and "me first." It is the same path that Jesus took. It's a path of humility, servanthood and giving life to others. And its downward motion insures heaven's rescue from evil!

Scripture – *"Your attitude should be the same as that of Christ Jesus: who, being in the very nature God, did not consider equality with God something to be grasped, but made himself nothing, taking the very nature of a servant, being made in human likeness. And being found in appearance as a man, he humbled himself and became obedient to death – even death on a cross! Therefore God exalted him to highest place and gave him the name that is above every name."* Philippians 2:5-11

Prayer – Dear Father, I am comforted today by the truth that I can follow in the footsteps of Jesus. Help me to realize that through my own strength I will surely fail, but when I rely on the ways of Christ, You will be exalted, and I will find my place in You. In Jesus' name, Amen.

Day 192

God Promotes

A Truth to Live – God's chosen path of humility and servanthood may look to some like a step backward. But rest assured that God's ways are better and higher. God alone can give a lasting reward, an eternal promotion that begins in the here and now and goes on, forever.

Scripture – *"Your attitude should be the same as that of Christ Jesus: who, being in the very nature God, did not consider equality with God something to be grasped, but made himself nothing, taking the very nature of a servant, being made in human likeness. And being found in appearance as a man, he humbled himself and became obedient to death – even death on a cross! Therefore God exalted him to highest place and gave him the name that is above every name."* Philippians 2:5-11

Prayer – Heavenly Lord, You have described the best way for me to live. Simple. Honest. Dependent on You. Help me to trust in Your future and to remember today that You are the one who promotes and exalts. I will look to You, and You alone, for my reward. In Jesus' name, Amen.

Day 193

The Fast Track to Greatness

A Truth to Live – God's path to greatness has clearly defined boundaries. True greatness in God's eyes is found when I serve the needs, ambitions and dreams of others. The world's upside down view is self-promoting, but God's ways are about honoring others.

Scripture – *"Whoever wants to become great among you must be your servant, and whoever wants to be first must be your slave – just as the Son of Man did not come to be served, but to serve, and to give his life as a ransom for many."* Matthew 20:26-28

Prayer – Heavenly Father, today I commit to walk Your path of servanthood. Help me to cease from striving for my own gain or recognition and instead find ways to make those around me shine. In honoring others I will honor You. In Jesus' name, Amen.

Day 194

It's Time to Serve

A Truth to Live – God's path to greatness begins with a shift in the attitude of my heart. The expectations of leadership in the world's eyes come with privilege, but true leadership before God begins with serving others.

Scripture – *"Whoever wants to become great among you must be your servant, and whoever wants to be first must be your slave – just as the Son of Man did not come to be served, but to serve, and to give his life as a ransom for many."* Matthew 20:26-28

Prayer – God in Heaven, I trust You and the path that You have designed for me. Help me to stop seeking privilege and position and begin to find ways to humble myself and serve others. In Jesus' name, Amen.

Day 195

Others First

A Truth to Live – When I am frustrated by the lack of respect I receive from others, I am going to stop demanding my "rights" and use the opportunity to give honor and respect to others. God's ways always put other's first.

Scripture – *"Love must be sincere. Hate what is evil; cling to what is good. Be devoted to one another in brotherly love. Honor one another above yourselves.* Romans 12: 9-10

Prayer – Heavenly Father, teach me today to put others first. Rather than prove myself or demand a position of honor from others, I will instead use every opportunity today to honor others first. In Jesus' name, Amen.

Day 196

Practice Hospitality

A Truth to Live – God's ways are perfect. Every time. Instead of demanding that I become an expert in the Bible, He simply asks me to humbly open my home and my life to others. When I demonstrate my love for God and others I shine the brightest.

Scripture – "*Share with God's people who are in need. Practice hospitality.*" Romans 12:13

Prayer – Lord, today I will choose to open up my heart and my life for others. Help me not to become overly concerned that I would have the perfect answers or impress others. Instead, use me to share Your love with others. In Jesus' name, Amen.

Day 197

It's Time to Do Right

A Truth to Live – Living out God's best requires that I do what is right every time. Even when other's actions are evil, I am to be careful to do right and to live at peace with others.

Scripture – *"Do not repay anyone evil for evil. Be careful to do what is right in the eyes of everybody. If it is possible, as far as it depends on you, live at peace with everyone."* Romans 12:16-18

Prayer – Dear Father, today I will choose to do what is right. Even when others may respond in ways that are hurtful I commit to follow You and spread Your peace to those around me. I will trust You to lead down the right path. In Jesus' name, Amen.

Day 198

Build Others First

A Truth to Live – Leadership in God's world is not about getting ahead or proving that I am worth more than the next person. Jesus modeled a life that put others first and served those around Him so that they would excel in life. I should build others up like Jesus did.

Scripture – *"He gave some to be apostles, some to be prophets, some to be evangelists, and some to be pastors and teachers, to prepare God's people for works of service, so that the body of Christ may be built up."* Ephesians 4:1-12

Prayer – Dear Father, I ask today that You would help me to shift the focus of my attention away from personal success and toward helping others to achieve all that You have designed for them. Teach me to humble myself that others might see Your kindness in me. In Jesus' name, Amen.

Day 199

Lead in the Right Direction

A Truth to Live – God's intention is for me to lead others in the right direction. Not only are His plans perfect and for my good, but they also have the added benefit of using me as an instrument of His amazing handiwork.

Scripture – *"He gave some to be apostles, some to be prophets, some to be evangelists, and some to be pastors and teachers, to prepare God's people for works of service, so that the body of Christ may be built up."* Ephesians 4:1-12

Prayer – Heavenly Father, today I ask to be given an increased leadership responsibility in Your church. I realize that this means that there are certain character qualities in me that You want to improve, and I give You permission to mold me and transform me further into Your image. In Jesus' name, Amen.

Day 200

Submission Brings Peace

A Truth to Live – God's plan for me includes more than learning from Him and leading others down His path. Real peace comes when I balance my own responsibility to lead with an equal responsibility to follow. God has designed a spiritual authority in my life to help me become more like Him.

Scripture – *"He gave some to be apostles, some to be prophets, some to be evangelists, and some to be pastors and teachers, to prepare God's people for works of service, so that the body of Christ may be built up."* Ephesians 4:1-12

Prayer – Dear Father, I trust You today. Help me to understand those whom You have put in my life. Help me to be a learner and to open my heart and mind to those who have been put into my life to help me become more like You. In Jesus' name, Amen.

Day 201

There is a Better Way

A Truth to Live – God's plan for me is perfect. He knows every detail of my past, understands my present circumstance and foresees my future. He created it all, and He has carved a path out for my success. The better way is just one word: love.

Scripture – *"Love one another as I have loved you. By this all men will know that you are my disciples, if you love one another."* John 13:34-35

Prayer – Heavenly Father, teach me to trust You today. I know that Your plans for me are good and for my benefit. Help me to learn to express my love for You by choosing to love others. In Jesus' name, Amen.

Day 202

The Best Way

A Truth to Live – There is a single purpose that is designed to demonstrate to the entire world that Jesus Christ is the Redeemer of humankind. It is also the "sign" that others will know if someone is following Jesus as a disciple. That purpose and sign is a commitment of love one to another.

Scripture – *"Love one another as I have loved you. By this all men will know that you are my disciples, if you love one another."* John 13:34-35

Prayer – Eternal Father, help me to find practical ways today to show my love to You by loving others. I will turn away from selfish practices and choose instead to bless others ahead of my own needs and desires. In Jesus' name, Amen.

Day 203

He's the Conductor, I Am the Instrument

A Truth to Live – As the Creator and Sustainer of the universe God has every detail orchestrated. Every detail. He knows when the sun will rise, when the stars will brighten the night sky and every moment in between. The best news is that He chose me to be a part of His plan to reveal His goodness to others.

Scripture – *"So in Christ we who are many form one body, and each member belongs to all the others. We have different gifts, according to the grace given us. If a man's gift is prophesying, let him use it in proportion to his faith. If it is serving, let him serve; if it is teaching, let him teach; if it is encouraging, let him encourage; if it is contributing to the needs of others, let him give generously; if it is leadership, let him govern diligently; if it is showing mercy, let him do it cheerfully."* Romans 12:5-8

Prayer – God, you are incredibly amazing. I realize today that You created me for a reason, a great purpose. And I choose to use the gifts and talents that I have been given to be a blessing and an encouragement to others. Help me today to learn that You are the Source, and I am part of Your grand plan. In Jesus' name, Amen.

Day 204

God is Not Done

A Truth to Live – When God created the earth and everything in it, He wasn't done. He is still creating good things, healing and restoring people, rescuing them from the dark side and using people to extend His blessing.

Scripture – *"Now to each one the manifestation of the Spirit is given for the common good. To one there is given through the Spirit the message of wisdom, to another the message of knowledge by means of the same Spirit, to another faith by the same Spirit, to another gifts of healing by that one Spirit, to another miraculous powers, to another prophecy, to another distinguishing between spirits, to another speaking in different tongues, and to still another the interpretation of tongues. All these are the work of one and the same Spirit, and he gives them to each one, just as he determines."* 1 Corinthians 12:7

Prayer – Almighty and Generous God, today I join You to bring good to those around me. Use me through the power of Your Spirit to break into the brokenness and pain of those around me and bring supernatural healing, blessing and abundance. In Jesus' name, Amen.

Day 205

The Power of Group Think

A Truth to Live – God knows that people need one another. He has deposited His gifts/talents and skills in each of us so that when we work together we complement each other's abilities, strengthen weak areas and experience God's goodness. His plan for me includes being a part of a God-group.

Scripture – "*Everyone has a hymn, or a word of instruction, a revelation, a tongue or an interpretation. All of these must be done for the strengthening of the church.*" I Corinthians 14:26

Prayer – Dear Father, I know that Your best for me includes belonging to a group of believers who trust You and honor each other. I ask that You grant me the courage to invest in these relationships and raise my expectations of Your Holy Spirit moving powerfully to bring wholeness to all. In Jesus' name, Amen.

Day 206

The "Must Have" Gift

A Truth to Live – God's plan for me is to be filled with His goodness, His presence and His power. He loves me so much that He doesn't want me to go through life on my own. He has left me His written Word, but also promises to fill me with His unquenchable power to demonstrate His love to others.

Scripture – *"Wait for the gift my Father has promised...you will receive power when the Holy Spirit comes on you; and you will be my witnesses in Jerusalem, and in all Judea and Samaria, and to the ends of the earth."* Acts 1:4, 8

Prayer – Great Giver of Gifts, Father in Heaven today I asked to be filled, baptized, immersed and renewed in the power of the Holy Spirit. I can see that in my every day decisions and actions I need more than what I have, and I ask You for the power to be a witness for You. In Jesus' name, Amen.

Day 207

It's Time!

A Truth to Live – God is the fuel behind every good thing I do. In fact, His plans to redeem the world begin with me! Since He is about real transformation that is much more than splash and sizzle, God wants to change me for the better and then help me extend the blessing to those around me.

Scripture – *"Go and make disciples of all nations, baptizing them in the name of the Father and of the Son and of the Holy Spirit, and teaching them to obey everything I have commanded you."*
Matthew 28:19-20

Prayer – Eternal God, how grateful I am today that You are the fuel to keep me going. Today I commit to extend the incredible blessings You have given to me. Help me pass them along, finding open hearts and listening ears to share Your mercies and teach Your ways. In Jesus' name, Amen.

Day 208

The Kingdom of Peace

A Truth to Live – God's plan to restore hope and dignity begins with a generous offer of permanent peace that overcomes conflict, anxiety and tension. God's peace surpasses each and every "stress" point and provides lasting communion and connection with God.

Scripture – Say "*peace to each house. If a man of peace is there, your peace will rest on him; if not, it will return to you. Stay in that house, eating and drinking whatever they give you. Heal the sick who are there and tell them, 'the kingdom of God is near you'.*" Luke 10:1-11

Prayer – Jesus, You are the Prince of Peace. You grant Your permanent peace to those whose focus remains on You. Help me, Savior, to fix my gaze on You and to bring Your peace to those around me today. In Jesus' name, Amen.

Day 209

The Reason

A Truth to Live – God has a plan to restore and redeem the nations of the earth. As complex and difficult as the world around me seems, His plan is simple. God desires to transform me into a powerful witness of His glory - and then? God will use me to bring His light and hope to those around me.

Scripture – *"The reason the Son of God appeared was to destroy the devil's work."* 1 John 3:8

Prayer – Heavenly Father, Your plan to redeem people from every tongue, tribe and nation begins with me. Fill me today with Your purity and power so that I can expand Your kingdom in my family, friends, my community and the nations. In Jesus' name, Amen.

Day 210

God-sized Protection

A Truth to Live – I live in a battle zone. On the dark side are the minions and dastardly thoughts of evil, but on God's side there is light, love and the provision to grow each day . When I choose God's side – loving what He loves and doing what His Son Jesus did – God rushes in to protect and guide me.

Scripture – *"Loose the chains of injustice set the oppressed free, share our food with the hungry and provide shelter and clothing to the poor."* It is only then that we can expect that our *"light will break forth like the dawn, and our healing will quickly appear; our righteousness will go before us, and the glory of the Lord will be your rear guard.*" Isaiah 58:6-9

Prayer – Gracious Father, today I choose to be on Your side, to love what You love and do what I see You doing. Help me to receive freely from You and to give freely to others. In Jesus' name, Amen.

Day 211

Is it Over?

A Truth to Live – Every day newscasters, prophets, and prognosticators predict the end. Some say it is eminent, other claim that it is soon, or perhaps just a few weeks, months or years away. But God has a pre-determined plan when it comes to the "end."

Scripture – *"And this gospel of the Kingdom has been preached in all the world as a testimony to all nations, the end will come."* Matthew 24:14

Prayer – Gracious Father, how grateful I am to know the parameters You have set for the closing of history. I will join in Your grand plan to see the Gospel preached in all the world – a concrete and evident plan to every ethnic group in the world. Help me to join what Your church is doing to proclaim Your name in all the earth. In Jesus' name, Amen.

Day 212

It's Time to Look Up

A Truth to Live – It is easy to look down and be down, especially when the daily news around us is negative or ominous. But God tells me to look up and to trust in His ultimate plan of redemption. He is good and He is God. He is in control and He has my best interest in mind. My day will go better with Him in charge.

Scripture – *"Stand up and lift up our heads, because our Redemption is drawing near."* Luke 21:28

Prayer – Eternal Father, I trust in Your plan. You were there before the world began, and You will see it through past the end. So when news around me turns gloomy or negative remind me to stand up, to look up and to watch for You. You promise to be there with me now, and come for me again. I am waiting for You, Lord. In Jesus' name, Amen.

Day 213

God's Mission, My Passion

A Truth to Live – The absolute best choice I can ever make is to follow hard after God. Pursuing His mission in my life means that I focus my time, my talents, my treasures and my future on God's ultimate plan. When I seek after Him, He rewards me with a life filled with blessings!

Scripture – *"And without faith it is impossible to please God, because anyone who comes to him must believe that He exists and that He rewards those who earnestly seek Him."* Hebrews 1:6

Prayer – Gracious and Merciful Father, I know that You are God eternal and that Your plans are good. I believe that You were, that You are, and that You will be. Grant to me the privilege of joining You in Your great mission on the earth. In Jesus' name, Amen.

Day 214

God's Kingdom is My Home

A Truth to Live – The best way to resist the many distractions that life can bring is to choose my final destination. I should never allow the confusion and "dead-end" promises of this world to keep me from crossing the finish line with a job well done. God promises to reward every person who seeks after His righteousness and His kingdom.

Scripture – "*But seek first his kingdom and his righteousness, and all these things will be given to you as well.*" Matthew 6:33

Prayer – Eternal Father, I commit today that Your Kingdom is my daily desire and my final destination. I will work with all my effort to see Your Kingdom come here and to live a life worthy of Your forgiveness, knowing that one day I will receive every blessing promised in Your Word. In Jesus' name, Amen.

Day 215

All Things New

A Truth to Live – When Jesus said, "*Behold, I make all things new*" (Revelation 21:5) His promise was certain and true. Only Jesus can make everything that was - new. He can take a tattered, beaten and wounded heart and make it fresh and clean. Help me to cling to this eternal promise and allow Jesus to make something new of me.

Scripture – "*He who was seated on the throne said, 'I am making everything new!'*" Revelation 21:5

Prayer – Dear Jesus, I surrender my past to You and ask You to make me brand new: clean, focused on You. Grant to me a fresh start. In Your name I pray, Amen.

Day 216

The Pursuit of Prayer

A Truth to Live – More than formulas and repetition, real prayer is about pursuing God. At its deepest level prayer is a humble admission that I am not in control and that He is. That's why pursuing God in prayer is the best way to start my day.

Scripture – *"O God, you are my God, earnestly I seek you; my soul thirsts for you, my body longs for you, in a dry and weary land where there is no water."* Psalm 63:1

Prayer – God, teach me to hunger after You each and every day. I put You in complete control of my day. In Jesus' name, Amen.

Day 217

The Centerpiece of Worship

A Truth to Live – Following Jesus requires much more than sparing an hour each week or providing finances to a worthy cause. God designed me to live to my fullest when God moves from the sidelines to the center of my life.

Scripture – *"Give honor to the LORD for the glory of his name. Worship the LORD in the splendor of his holiness."* Psalm 29:2

Prayer – Heavenly Father, today I move You from the periphery to the very center of my life. I will worship You with my whole being – my body, mind and spirit. In Jesus' name, Amen.

Day 218

A Light in the Darkness

A Truth to Live – Finding my way in this complex world can be simple. Simple? Yes, when I choose to base my life on the powerful truth of God's Word and not on the comments or circumstances around me.

Scripture – "*Your word is a lamp to my feet and a light for my path.*" Psalm 119:105

Prayer – Heavenly Father, You have come to help rescue me from darkness. Today I choose to base the direction of my life on Your Word knowing that its Truth will prevail in Jesus' name, Amen.

Day 219

Strength in Solitude

A Truth to Live – The best way to find solutions to life's problems is to spend more time with God – alone. When I choose to step away from the noise created by the opinions of others and find refuge in God and His Word, my future is sealed in God.

Scripture – *"God is our refuge and strength, an ever-present help in trouble."* Psalm 46:1

Prayer – Lord, today I will carve out more time to be with You and seek You with all my heart. You alone will be my strength. In Jesus' name, Amen.

Day 220

Pleasing Meditation

A Truth to Live – I can have a heart and mind that is focused, strong, clear and pleasing to God. It begins with a simple and bold decision to find a quiet space and soak in the truths of God's Word.

Scripture – *"May the words of my mouth and the meditation of my heart, be pleasing in your sight O Lord, my Rock and my Redeemer."* Psalm 19:14

Prayer – Heavenly Father, today I will set aside time to quiet my mind and heart and focus on You. Help me to place Your Word as my guiding light so that my life is pleasing to You. In Jesus' name, Amen.

Day 221

Finding a Breakthrough

A Truth to Live – In simple words, fasting is choosing to do without and focusing on being with God. I can do without food, entertainment or anything else that has a grip on my attention.

Scripture – "*Even now," declares the Lord, "return to me with all your heart, with fasting and weeping and mourning." Return to the Lord your God, for he is gracious and compassionate, slow to anger and abounding in love, and he relents from sending calamity."* Joel 2:12-13

Prayer – Father in Heaven, today I turn the focus of my life toward You. You are the source of my joy and the sustenance of my life. I will choose, in some small way, to sacrifice food or pleasure so that I can spend more time with You. Renew my heart, I pray. In Jesus' name, Amen.

Day 222

Keep it Simple

A Truth to Live – Love God. Love your neighbor. That's it. When they asked Jesus what the greatest commandment was, he replied:

Scripture – *"Love the Lord your God with all your heart and with all your soul and with all your mind. This is the first and greatest commandment. And the second is like it: Love your neighbor as yourself."* Matthew 22:37

Prayer – Dear Lord, I choose to be passionate about You today. Your interests and desires will be mine. I will make You first. To demonstrate my allegiance to You, I will also love the one next to me. All day. In Jesus' name, Amen.

Day 223

Repentance

A Truth to Live – Tired and fatigued? The answer might be as simple as turning toward God. Most people use the word "repentance" to turn away from something. While this true, what if I started thinking of repentance as turning toward God?

Scripture – *"Repent then, and turn to God, so that your sins may be wiped out, that times of refreshing may come from the Lord."* Acts 3:19

Prayer – Dear Lord, I am turning toward You today. I will walk away from the habits and behavior that create stress, fatigue and frustration in my heart. Meet me today with Your mercy and Your love. In Jesus' name, Amen.

Day 224

The Right Side

A Truth to Live – Finding contentment each day has to do with making the right choices. The small choices that I make throughout the day go a long way toward creating an environment that is stress-free and filled with contentment. Being on God's side of the issues and events is what opens the way for healing and cleansing.

Scripture – *"If you confess [stand with God's view over each circumstance] your sin, he is faithful and just and will forgive us our sins, and purify us from all unrighteousness.* 1 John 1:9

Prayer – Dear Father, today I will focus on making right choices throughout the day. When I fall short, I will view my decisions and actions through the lens of Your Word. As I see things the way You do, then I know that my heart and mind will be cleansed from impurity, stress and unbelief. I am standing with You! In Jesus' name, Amen.

Day 225

Restoration or Retaliation?

A Truth to Live – Rather than pretending that a conflict doesn't exist or that there are no "issues" between family and friends, God wants me to repair my broken relationships using the principle of restitution. When I have taken something from someone, or wronged them in any way, I should work to restore the relationship rather than retaliate.

Scripture – *"When a man or woman wrongs another in any way and so is unfaithful to the Lord, that person is guilty 7 and must confess the sin he has committed. He must make full restitution for his wrong, add one fifth to it and give it all to the person he has wronged."* Numbers 5:5-7

Prayer – Dear Lord, I have asked You many times to forgive me and cleanse me from wrong, but somehow find it difficult to forgive others. You are asking me to forgive and restore back the things that have been broken. Today I commit to obey Your Word. Grant me the strength to re-connect broken relationships and find ways to offer complete restitution. In Jesus' name, Amen.

Day 226

Parenting

A Truth to Live – Beyond all the self-help books and tips about child rearing is it really possible to raise a child destined to be a "champion" in today's world? Without a vital relationship with God and belonging to a vibrant community of believers it is very difficult.

Scripture – *"Train a child in the way he should go, and when he is old he will not turn from it."*
Proverbs 22:6

Prayer – Dear Father, today I turn to You. I will choose to be led daily by the wisdom of Your Word so that I can learn what it means to be "trained." As I learn from You I will, in turn, apply these truths in my family. Help me to be faithful and honest with a community of believers so that my children will grow to fear You and glorify Your name in name in all the earth. In Jesus' name, Amen.

Day 227

Together

A Truth to Live – God has designed me to go through life with others. He even created me with certain limitations to help me recognize that my needs can only be met through an interdependent relationship with others! Followers of Christ call this "togetherness" church, and find meaning by serving God and one another's needs. Many people are confused and think that the church exists to meet their needs when just the opposite is true. The church exists so that I can serve others and meet their needs.

Scripture – *"Let us not give up meeting together, as some are in the habit of doing, but let us encourage one another – and all the more as you see the Day approaching."* Hebrews 10:25

Prayer – Dear Heavenly Father, today I recognize that the cure for my loneliness and lack of meaning is found in serving the needs of others. Help me to follow Your plan and look for opportunities to bless others. I commit to meet and grow together with others who are a part of my church family. I believe that You will meet my own needs when I help meet the needs of others. In Jesus' name, Amen.

Day 228

A Learner

A Truth to Live – The best teachers are always learners. The best parents are learners. The best players are learners. The best workers are learners. The best musicians are learners. Get the point? It's about positioning myself to learn and grow. The Bible calls it discipleship, and Jesus asks us to be a disciple and to make disciples.

Scripture – *"Therefore go and make disciples of all nations."* Matthew 28:19

Prayer – Eternal Father and Master Teacher, I recognize my need to learn from You today. Help me to not become so self-reliant that I neglect to ask You for wisdom, insight and direction for my day. I desire to learn from You and to share with others what I am learning. Help me to be a disciple and to make disciples – followers and learners of You. In Jesus' name, Amen.

Day 229

How Many Times?

A Truth to Live – Sometimes the hardships of life cripple my emotions and cause great pain. The easiest thing to do is build a defense mechanism that can be filled with resentment, bitterness and cynicism. In the end this never works. But Jesus has provided an alternative for my total healing. It's called forgiveness.

Scripture – *"Then Peter came to Jesus and asked, 'Lord how many times shall I forgive my brother when he sins against me? Seven times?' Jesus answered, 'I tell you, not seven times, but 490 times'."*
Matthew 18:21-22

Prayer – Heavenly Father, You have forgiven me so many times. Thank You! I admit to You that sometimes I do not have the emotional strength to forgive those who have hurt me. But today, I receive Your forgiveness for my sins and I, in turn, will forgive those who have wounded my heart. May Your forgiving power restore my soul. In Jesus' name, Amen.

Day 230

The Spoken Word

A Truth to Live – My words have the power to hurt and the power to heal. They can encourage and lift up or tear down and destroy. One word can change the course of a conversation or build momentum to accomplish the unthinkable. My words have power.

Scripture – *"May the words of my mouth and the meditation of my heart be pleasing in your sight O Lord, my Rock and my Redeemer."* Psalm 19:14

Prayer – Father in heaven, today I ask for the strength to be quiet when needed, to encourage often and to gain control of my words throughout the day. Help me to speak life and hope into each moment of my day so that my words are pleasing to You. In Jesus' name.

Day 231

Greatness

A Truth to Live – The push toward success is everywhere. But success in what? In the eyes of others? In my own eyes? What about success in God's eyes? Isn't that what I should be aiming for?

Scripture – *"Whoever wants to become great among you must be your servant."* Matthew 20:26

Prayer – Eternal Father, teach me today to walk in humility, preferring others and not insisting on my own way. Help me to see that greatness in Your Kingdom is measured by the depth of my service toward others. Grant me an opportunity to serve someone today. In Jesus' name, Amen.

Day 232

Giving

A Truth to Live – I know, like every farmer knows, that I must first plant a seed before I can expect a harvest. In relationships the principle is the same: if I want to have a friend I must be a friend. My relationship with God is no different. I must give my heart to God before I can receive new life in Him.

Scripture – *"Give, and it will be given to you. A good measure, pressed down, shaken together and running over will be poured into your lap. For with the measure you use, it will be measured to you."*
Luke 6:38

Prayer – Dear Father, You have modeled to me what it means to be generous and giving. You breathed life into this universe, gave Your only Son for my salvation and You give the presence of Your Holy Spirit for those who follow You. I am choosing today to give. I will become a generous and giving person, focused on the needs of others rather than myself. As I give to others I know that You will be faithful to provide for my every need. In Jesus' name, Amen.

Day 233

It's Time to Serve

A Truth to Live – Everyday people find hope and meaning when they serve others. There is something special that takes place in my mind and heart when I turn my attention away from my own personal needs and toward meeting the needs of others. It is better to give than to receive.

Scripture – *"Jesus came to this earth from heaven not to be served, but to serve."* Matthew 20:28

Prayer – Dear Lord, today I will take steps to follow Your lead. Rather than focus on what I think I deserve, I will begin today concentrating on what You deserve and what others need. I will choose to serve rather than be served and, in doing so, I believe that Your presence will grow in my life. In Jesus' name, Amen.

Day 234

Humility

A Truth to Live – Humility becomes a reality in my life when I have a very realistic picture of who God is, who others are and who I am. Honor comes to those who recognize the gifts and skills of others and praise them above their own. Why? Because God exalts those who humble themselves.

Scripture – *"Humble yourselves before the Lord, and he will lift you up."* James 4:7

Prayer – Dear Lord, sometimes I find it difficult to humble myself in front of others. But even when others are fighting for their position I will choose to humble myself before You and leave my destiny in Your hands. Grant me the strength to take the first step and prefer others before myself. In Jesus' name, Amen.

Day 235

Obedience

A Truth to Live – There is only one complete manual about life. It is filled with practical instruction and wisdom for every imaginable circumstance. In it I can find answers about relationships, finances, work, study, devotion and much more. Perhaps the most important lesson it teaches is the simple lesson of obedience.

Scripture – *"By [God's word] is your servant warned; in keeping [his word] there is great reward."*
Psalm 19:11

Prayer – Dear Lord, I promise to read Your Word today because I know that the Bible provides for me a path to life. Please grant to me the revelation and understanding that I need so that I can apply Your wisdom to my life. Teach me to obey Your Word that I might receive the great reward of Your presence every moment of my life. In Jesus' name, Amen.

Day 236

It's Time to Go

A Truth to Live – Jesus' last words on this earth were a call to action. He told His disciples to "go" and "make disciples" of all ethnic peoples in the world. When I put into action what I believe it changes me, and it changes those around me. In this case, Jesus asked his disciples to make disciples – obedient followers of Jesus' teachings.

Scripture – *"Go and make disciples of all nations, baptizing them in the name of the Father and of the Son and of the Holy Spirit, and teaching them to obey everything I have commanded you."*
Matthew 28:19-20

Prayer – Dear Father, today I commit to put Your divine words into action in my life. I will follow You with all that I am; and I will teach others to obey what You have commanded. In that I know Your blessings will surround me. In Jesus' name, Amen.

Day 237

The Gift Giver

A Truth to Live – Jesus' is a gift giver. He gave His life, and when I follow Him He grants to me supernatural gifts to make His name known. The "gifts of the spirit" are designed to bring revelation to my day, insight and wisdom to those around me and direction for my future. I have been given access to live a heaven-inspired life right now.

Scripture – *"Now to each one the manifestation of the Holy Spirit is given for the common good."*
1 Corinthians12: 7

Prayer – Father in Heaven, how incredibly gracious You are to grant to me today Your supernatural gifts. I will begin my day asking for Your direction and for the impartation of Your supernatural gifts to be evident in my life. I commit to use these gifts for the good of others. In Jesus' name, Amen.

Day 238

A Story to Tell

A Truth to Live – The gift of eternal life that I have been offered in Christ (John 1:12) is far greater than the generosity of any man. Forgiveness, peace and the joy of God's presence are just the beginnings of a life of meaning and purpose. The transforming power of God is worth sharing with others!

Scripture – *"How can they call on the one they have not believed in? And how can they believe in the one of whom they have not heard? And how can they hear without someone preaching to them?* Romans 10:14

Prayer – Dear Father, You have done so much for me, and I ask today for the privilege to share in some small way Your great gift of life with others. Grant me the courage to communicate how You have healed and transformed me from the inside out. In Jesus' name, Amen.

Day 239

Healing

A Truth to Live – So much of life is lived out between the difficulties of "coping" and heroic efforts of "overcoming." But life with Jesus can point me in a different direction. Rather than coping with hidden pain or mustering up the strength to overcome the "issues" that confront me, Jesus offers the opportunity to be transformed AND to walk in a way that transforms others.

Scripture – *"He called his twelve disciples to him and gave them authority to drive out evil spirits and to heal every disease and sickness."* Matthew 10:1

Prayer – Dear Father, today I desire to move past coping with, or even struggling to overcome, the emotional "issues" that surround my past and present. Instead I am turning to Your Son, Jesus, and asking for healing that can radically transform me. I also am asking for the boldness to walk in Your authority so that as I am healed I will be able to bring Your transforming power to those around me. In Jesus' name, Amen.

Day 240

Deliver Me From Evil

A Truth to Live – There is a difference between right and wrong and good and evil. Many people today are too timid to speak of the reality of an evil force, but Jesus even mentioned the force of evil in the Lord's Prayer: "*lead us not into temptation but deliver us from evil.*" The power of God can deliver me from the forces of the evil one!

Scripture – *He called his twelve disciples to him and gave them authority to drive out evil spirits and to heal every disease and sickness."* Matthew 10:1

Prayer – Lord, You alone have the power, might and dominion to overcome evil. I know that the reason You came to this world was to destroy the works of the evil one. Today I receive the authority that You have granted to submit to You, resist the influence of evil and to drive evil away from my life in Jesus name, Amen.

Day 241

Just Serve One

A Truth to Live – The desire for more in this world is a never-ending trap of materialism, disappointment and despair. Perhaps this is why the Scripture says that the *"love of money is the root of all evil."* (I Timothy 6:10) One of the simplest and profound ways to serve God is to loosen the grip that money has on my life.

Scripture – *"No one can serve two masters. Either he will hate the one and love the other, or he will be devoted to the one and despise the other. You cannot serve both God and money."* Matthew 6:24

Prayer – Dear Lord, for too long I have attempted to juggle my loyalties between You and the pleasures of this world. I see now that I need to stop pursuing pleasures and pursue You whole-heartedly. You alone are my treasure and my priority. Today I release control of my material possessions and promise to use them as a blessing for Your kingdom. In Jesus' name, Amen.

Day 242

Do Justice

A Truth to Live – Following God's ways is a journey of choices and actions. The choices are what I believe and the actions are how I live out what I believe. Jesus compared it to the fruit of tree. You can tell the type of tree based on the fruit it bears. One evidence of God's journey is acting "justly" and giving mercy to others.

Scripture – *"He has shown you, O man, what is good. And what does the Lord require of you? To act justly, and to love mercy and to walk humbly with your God."* Micah 6:8

Prayer – Heavenly Father, I realize that to walk with You I must carry out justice in my world. It is not sufficient for me to see the dark impact of evil in this world and complain. Grant me the courage and wisdom to begin to defend those whose lives are mistreated and to work for justice for those who remain defenseless. In Jesus' name, Amen.

Day 243

Into all the World

A Truth to Live – The Gospel of Jesus Christ is so incredible that it needs to be shared with everyone everywhere. In fact, the Gospel of Matthew declares that when every ethnic group in the world has heard the Good News, Jesus will come back!

Scripture – "*Go and make disciples of all the ethnic groups of the world, baptizing them in the name of the Father and of the Son and of the Holy Spirit, and teaching them to obey everything I have commanded you.*" Matthew 28:19

Prayer – Dear Heavenly Father, today I will join the effort of sharing the Good News to the entire world; to every country; and to every ethnic people. You deserve to be worshipped among all peoples! Give me a heart for those that are unreached with the Good News, and show me what I can do to be a part of declaring Your name among the nations. In Jesus name, Amen.

Day 244

Anticipation

A Truth to Live – I know that Jesus is coming back. The Bible says that every person who calls on His name, trusts in Him, and walks in His ways will be saved. But when is He coming? No one knows for sure but my heart can grow in anticipation when I see an increase in extreme violence, war and natural disasters. These are "signs of the times."

Scripture – Jesus said, *"When these things begin to take place, stand up and lift your heads, because your redemption is drawing near."* Luke 21:28

Prayer – Jesus, today I will allow my heart to grow in anticipation for Your soon-coming return. You will right all wrong, bless those who follow You and redeem all of us back to Yourself. Help me to stay focused on You and share Your love with others. In Your name, Amen.

Day 245

Time to Change Direction

A Truth to Live – God's ways are higher, better and headed in a different direction. To truly experience God's best I must shift the focus of my attention away from what can make my life better and toward what will give glory and honor to Him.

Scripture – *"From that time on Jesus began to preach, "Repent, for the Kingdom of heaven is near."* Matthew 4:17

Prayer – God, you alone are King Eternal. You have been in charge, You are in charge, and You will be in charge. Help me to turn away from my own natural desires – and from the desires of the world around me – and to put my complete allegiance in You. I will devote myself to pleasing You. In Jesus' name, Amen.

Day 246

It's Big-Time Small

A Truth to Live – God's ways are not always noticeable and their beginnings are often small. But when patiently nurtured God's ways become strength, safety and wisdom for all those who rest in them.

Scripture – *"The kingdom of heaven is like a mustard seed, which a man took and planted in his field. Though it is the smallest of all seeds, yet when it grows, it is the largest of garden plants and becomes a tree, so that the birds of the air come and perch in its branches."* Matthew 13:31

Prayer – Heavenly King, all around me people are pursuing things that start big and seem to have temporary influence. I am so grateful that Your ways are opposite of the world. Your beginnings may be small but they last and provide wisdom and strength for others. Help me, Lord, to be used in some small way today to extend Your Kingdom. In Jesus' name, Amen.

Day 247

A Small Portion Makes a Big Impact

A Truth to Live – God's Kingdom is the invisible force that can shape conversations, family decisions, careers and the destiny of a nation. It works like the smallest portion of yeast in bread. Though small and easily overlooked its potent force brings life and beauty to everything it touches.

Scripture – *"The kingdom of heaven is like yeast that a woman took and mixed into a large amount of flour until it worked all through the dough."* Matthew 13:33

Prayer – Heavenly King, I am your subject and will follow and obey You at every turn. It is my desire to walk away from the need to be seen and instead to become like yeast – allowing You to work through me and in me as You will. I choose today to follow You and ask to be used to expand Your Kingdom. In Jesus' name, Amen.

Day 248

Finding Greatness in Complete Dependence

A Truth to Live – The world system teaches me to work toward financial and relational independence. But God desires just the opposite. He asks me to use the gifts and talents that I have been given for His purposes and to become completely dependent on Him.

Scripture – *"Who is the greatest in the kingdom of heaven? I tell you the truth, unless you change and become like little children you will never enter the kingdom of heaven."* Matthew 18:1-3

Prayer – Matchless Savior, help me to change today. I will no longer seek financial and relational independence in my life. Instead, I submit all that I have and all that I am to You. I will become completely dependent on You and on Your direction for my life, for my friends and family and for my future. Help me to use the things that I have been given to extend Your Kingdom. In Jesus' name, Amen.

Day 249

The First Are Last and the Last Are First

A Truth to Live – Our natural desire is to be first. We want to be first in line, first to finish, and first among our peers. But clearly this is not the way of Jesus' Kingdom. If I want to finish first in the view of eternity then I must choose to be last and defer to others ahead of myself.

Scripture – *"The Kingdom of Heaven is like a landowner who went out early in the morning to hire men in his vineyard. He agreed to pay a day's wage and sent them out. About the third hour, the sixth and the ninth hour he hired others and promised them a day's wage. When evening came he said, call the workers and pay them their wages, beginning with the last ones hired and going on to the first. So the last will be first and the first shall be last."*
Matthew 20:1-16

Prayer – Master, I will no longer seek to be first. Today I am choosing the way of Your Kingdom – seeking to do my best but to not insist that I am rewarded for a job well done. Help me to prefer others to get the credit above myself and in doing so put You first. In Jesus' name, Amen.

Day 250

The Big Discovery

A Truth to Live – Many believe that real power, wisdom and insight come from learning or listening to certain "authorities." But God's Kingdom comes through ultimate and complete surrender to the control and directive leading of God. When I receive Jesus Christ into my heart and yield control of all I am and do, then the Kingdom of God resides in me!

Scripture – *"The kingdom of God does not come with your careful observation, nor will people say, 'Here it is' or 'there it is,' because the Kingdom of God is within you."* Luke 17:21

Prayer – Dear Jesus, help me to stop trying to find that perfect "place" where I can experience You and to realize that You are already here and everywhere. Teach me to not pursue the latest fad of teaching or whims of doctrine in the hopes of finding You through some secret knowledge. I know that You are knocking on the door of my heart (Revelation 3:20) and want to come in and be with me. I yield control of who I am and choose to follow Your lead. In Jesus' name, Amen.

Day 251

Living Here But Serving There

A Truth to Live – The Kingdom of God is not of this world. Its values and principles are heavenly and always function in the opposite spirit of the "me first" worldview all around me. As a follower of Jesus, I am to live in this world but adhere to the principles of the Kingdom of God.

Scripture – *"My Kingdom is not of this world. If it were, my servants would fight to prevent my arrest by the Jews. But now my kingdom is from another place."* John 18:36

Prayer – Heavenly King, today I choose to belong to You, to follow Your ways and live in Your Kingdom. I recognize that too many times my relationship with You, God, and with others, centers on my needs. But from now on I want to be focused on bringing You glory and magnifying Your name in the earth. In Jesus' name, Amen.

Day 252

It's Coming!

A Truth to Live – The followers of Jesus asked Him one day to teach them to pray. His response spoke volumes about purpose and meaning in life. The entire mission of God on this earth is to bring the heavenly Kingdom of God to earth – through me. When I join His mission I find purpose and meaning for my life.

Scripture – *"Your Kingdom come, Your will be done, on earth as it is in heaven."* Matthew 6:10

Prayer – Mighty Redeemer, You have orchestrated history so that I have the privilege of joining Your mission. I will stop praying for my needs alone and, beginning today, make my priority in life Your mission on the earth. Your Kingdom come, Your will be done on earth as it is in heaven! In Jesus' name, Amen.

Day 253

Looking In All the Right Places

A Truth to Live – God has established the ground rules for me to find peace, harmony and purpose in my life. What's the most important "rule"? To seek God's Kingdom and His righteousness…then everything else I need will be added to me.

Scripture – *"Seek first His kingdom and His righteousness, and all these things will be given to you as well."* Matthew 6:33

Prayer – Father in Heaven, it seems that everywhere else I turn pundits, teachers and news broadcasters are pointing to the problems all around me and crises around the world. Help me to listen to Your Word and to follow Your truth. I will seek You today and Your righteousness and then rest in peace that Your peace and provision will follow me. In Jesus' name, Amen.

Day 254

It's Worth It All

A Truth to Live – The Kingdom of God is more valuable than everything I have. When I discover its worth, the only way to genuinely respond is to trade in every dream, ambition, goal and passion I have for the privilege of belonging to the Kingdom. Anything less disqualifies me.

Scripture – *"The Kingdom of heaven is like a treasure hidden in a field. When a man found it, he hid it again, and then in his joy went and sold all he had and bought that field."* Matthew 13:44

Prayer – Wonderful King, I am embarrassed to admit to You that for most of my life I have sought for answers and solutions to the problems that I face, without ever realizing that what I possess today pales in comparison to what You promise to provide for me. Today I trade in my hopes and dreams for Your Kingdom. Everything I say and do will ultimately be about You and Your purposes on the earth. In Jesus' name, Amen.

Day 255

The Greatest Value

A Truth to Live – The Kingdom of God is more desirable than a good name, success at home or even the accolades of friends and peers. God's Kingdom is more valuable than all the money and resources in the earth. When I decide to pursue what is most valued, God transforms my pursuit into a journey of hope and joy.

Scripture – *"The kingdom of heaven is like a merchant looking for fine pearls. When he found one of great value, he went away and sold everything he had and bought it."* Matthew 13:45-46

Prayer – Eternal Father, help me today to forsake the pursuit of dreams and plans that are meaningless and, instead focus my entire life on Your mission of bringing the Kingdom of Heaven to earth. I ask that You would bring others into my life that will help me remain focused and in pursuit of You. In Jesus' name, Amen.

Day 256

The Danger Zone

A Truth to Live – The most dangerous place to live is in the arena of self-sufficiency. It's the place where I "feel" like I can survive on my own. The best place to live is in total dependence on God. I can get out of the danger zone by giving away what I have and clinging to the life-line of God's Kingdom.

Scripture – *"I tell you the truth, it is hard for a rich man to enter the Kingdom of heaven. It is easier for a camel to go through the eye of a needle than for a rich man to enter the kingdom of God."* Matthew 19:23-24

Prayer – God, I ask today that You would rescue me from the danger zone of abundance. Place me in positions where I must remain completely dependent on You for everything that I need to live. In Jesus' name, Amen.

Day 257

Born Twice to Live Once

A Truth to Live – When I was brought into this world I immediately entered into a system of finite resources, limited love and partial peace. I was completely dependent on others. But to experience what God has for me – infinite blessings, complete love and total peace – I must be born again: Spiritual re-birth into His Kingdom!

Scripture – *"Jesus declared, "I tell you the truth, no one can see the Kingdom of God unless he is born again."* John 3:3

Prayer – Eternal Father, I live and breathe in a world that is limited and getting worse. Today I ask to be born again into Your Kingdom – a place of abundance, love and peace. I will no longer look to the world around me for direction; I will choose You and Your ways at every turn. In Jesus' name, Amen.

Day 258

Born into the Kingdom

A Truth to Live – Living and walking in the Kingdom of God requires a "departure" from one system and beginning life with God. It's more than just a new way of thinking or finding ways to incorporate the wisdom of God's Word into my current thoughts and actions. Entering the Kingdom of God is about leaving something that's old and broken and clinging to something that is new and life-giving.

Scripture – *"I tell you the truth, no one can enter the Kingdom of God unless he is born of water and the Spirit."* John 3:5

Prayer – Eternal Savior, thank You for extending Your mercy and grace to me. I ask that You would immerse me in Your love and cleanse me from sin. Baptize me in Your Spirit so that my thoughts and actions reflect Your Kingdom. In Jesus' name, Amen.

Day 259

Every Word Counts

A Truth to Live – Living within the boundaries and safety of the Kingdom of God becomes simple when I make Jesus the Supreme King of my life and I become His humble subject. Since His words breathe life into every situation, when I speak the Word of God, His Kingdom comes near.

Scripture – *"From that time on Jesus began to preach, 'Repent for the Kingdom of heaven is near'."*
Matthew 4:17

Prayer – Gracious and merciful Savior, How grateful I am for Your incredible love and forgiveness. Wash over me with the fountain of Your cleansing blood and create in me new passions for You. I commit to You today that the words of my mouth will speak only of Your truth and goodness to others. In Jesus' name, Amen.

Day 260

The Keys to Heaven

A Truth to Live – The King of Heaven has granted every follower the keys to His Kingdom. When I decide to follow Jesus the King, spiritual keys to His Kingdom are activated by words I speak and the life I live. God promises to watch over His Word to make sure it's completed (Jeremiah 1:12), so I will choose my words carefully. I will align myself with God's heart and watch the richness of His presence begin to shape my world.

Scripture – *"I will give you the keys of the Kingdom of heaven; whatever you bind on earth will be bound in heaven, and whatever you loose on earth will be loosed in heaven."* Matthew 16:19

Prayer – Eternally Good and Heavenly Father, Your kindness toward me is overwhelming. I will speak Your words of life today, knowing that they have the power to bind and loose – to protect and to free – my own life and those who hear Your Word. In Jesus' name, Amen.

Day 261

It's Not Over 'til It's Over

A Truth to Live – God has put me in the middle of His masterful plan for every ethnic group in the world – from the farthest flung tribal group to the urban masses next door – to hear the Good News before Jesus returns and establishes a new heaven and a new earth.

Scripture – *"And this gospel of the Kingdom will be preached in the whole world as a testimony to all nations [ethnic groups], and then the end will come."* Matthew 24:14

Prayer – God, You are an incredible Redeemer. I am amazed that You have chosen me to be a part of Your master plan to declare Your glory among all the ethnic groups of the world. Help me to see today that my words count for eternity and that You want me to invest in others who will join me in extending Your Kingdom. In Jesus' name, Amen.

Day 262

An Inheritance Too Big to Spend

A Truth to Live – Jesus, the King of Heaven measures true productivity. The Gospels tell numerous parables about workers being rewarded for their faithfulness and resourcefulness – and others being punished for their laziness. Every follower of Jesus may receive both a present tense and future reward for speaking the words of the Kingdom and bringing life to all who hear.

Scripture – *"Then the King will say to those on His right, 'Come you who are blessed by my Father; take your inheritance, the Kingdom prepared for you since the creation of the world'."* Matthew 25:34

Prayer – Heavenly Father, I come humbly to You today, acknowledging my own shortcomings and ask for You to grant me the strength and courage to speak Your words of life to others and to do Your will. I know that You have prepared an inheritance for those who follow You. Help me to follow You and You alone. In Jesus' name, Amen.

Day 263

It's Not Just for Me

A Truth to Live – Jesus, the One in charge of the Kingdom of Heaven, is on the move. He is always looking for those whose lives have been broken, shattered and wounded. The best way to "stay" in that sacred place of worship and healing with Jesus is to join Him on His continued mission.

Scripture – *"He said, 'I must preach the good news of the Kingdom of God to other towns also, because that is why I was sent.'"* Luke 4:43

Prayer – Righteous and Holy Father, help me today to follow You. I know that You spent Your life serving others, and I commit to follow in Your path. Help me to get past focusing on my own needs and recognize that You want to bless others through me. In Jesus' name, Amen.

Day 264

Let the Dead Bury the Dead

A Truth to Live – A pre-occupation with short-term material rewards is one of the biggest obstacles that keeps me from living and walking in richness of the Kingdom of God. I can overcome this temptation by speaking the words of life from the Scripture to everyone who crosses my path.

Scripture – *"Jesus said, 'Let the dead bury the dead, but you go and proclaim the Kingdom of God'."* Luke 9:60

Prayer – Eternal Leader, forgive me for turning my attention to the lifeless desires and appetites of the world. Help me today to change my behavior by proclaiming Your Kingdom with my words and speaking about the richness of Your Word to others. In Jesus' name, Amen.

Day 265

Driving out Demons

A Truth to Live – The Kingdom of God has more power than the grip of emotional wounds, addictive habits and the temptation of evil. The spiritual authority resident in Jesus is much more than a 'boost' used to personally improve my struggle against sin. The words of Jesus have the power to drive out the demons of hell and create a new life filled with peace.

Scripture – *"But if I drive out demons by the finger of God, then the Kingdom of God has come to you."* Luke 11:20

Prayer – O Great Rescuer, find me today and deliver me from the insanity of thinking that I can fix myself, or that by adding a few pearls of wisdom I can change my own behavior and destiny. You alone have the power over death and evil. May Your Kingdom come – now, and rescue me into Your permanent peace and wholeness. In Jesus' name, Amen.

Day 266

Joining the Mission of God

A Truth to Live – The invitation to *"come and follow me"* (Matthew 4:19) is extended from God to me each and every day. My "yes" to His call positions me to be with Him and also provides me with the Kingdom Power to be a part of His miraculous work.

Scripture – *"Jesus went through Galilee, teaching in their synagogues, preaching the good news of the Kingdom, and healing every disease and sickness among the people."* Matthew 4:23

Prayer – Today, Lord, I say "YES" to You. I will go with You today and join Your mission on the earth. Help me to confidently proclaim the Good News of the Kingdom and watch You deliver others from evil. In Jesus' name, Amen.

Day 267

Doing His Will

A Truth to Live – Every follower of Jesus is known, not so much by his words, but by his actions. I can say things I don't understand, or state things that I don't necessarily mean, but what I actually do shows what I believe. Joining the mission of God in Kingdom power is about doing and speaking His will.

Scripture – *"Not everyone who says to me, 'Lord, Lord' will enter the Kingdom of Heaven, but only he who does the will of my Father who is in heaven."* Matthew 7:21

Prayer – Gracious Father, today I commit to seek You, to follow You and to do Your will. Help me to listen before I act, to not be afraid of what others may think and to join Your mission by obeying Your Word in every circumstance. Grant me the courage to stay on course with You. In Jesus' name, Amen.

Day 268

Living Like Children

A Truth to Live – Healthy little children are care-free and filled with confidence and love for their parents. They trust their parents to provide for them, to guide them along the right path and to take care of their every need. I should follow Jesus with the same trust and freedom - knowing that joining His mission will keep me on the right path and provide all that I need.

Scripture – *"I tell you the truth, unless you change and become like little children, you will never enter the Kingdom of heaven."* Matthew18:3

Prayer – Heavenly Father, I trust You for everything that I need and for where I should go. I resign from being "in charge" of my own destiny and turn to You. By joining Your mission today, I am looking for You to lead me each step of my day and to show me Yourself in every circumstance. I will follow You. In Jesus' name, Amen.

Day 269

It's About the Fruit

A Truth to Live – Just like an apple tree produces apples so those who are on God's journey will produce spiritual fruit -- the character qualities and the actions that identify them with Jesus. When I join the mission of God with Kingdom power my life will bear good fruit.

Scripture – *"Therefore I tell you that the Kingdom of God will be taken away from you and given to people who will produce its fruit."* Matthew 21:43

Prayer – Gracious Father, help me today to follow You. I want to be known by You and those around me to be someone who produces the fruit of righteousness and who demonstrates Kingdom power. Grant to me the richness of Your presence and the potency of Your wisdom to both be and act according to Your will. In Jesus' name, Amen.

Day 270

Whatever It Takes

A Truth to Live – Joining the mission of God in Kingdom power requires a total and complete devotion to God and God alone. I must commit to avoid all temptations and distractions that would hinder my walk with God and keep me from completing the mission God has given me.

Scripture – "*And if your eye causes you to sin, pluck it out. It is better for you to enter the Kingdom of God with one eye than to have two eyes and be thrown into hell.*" Mark 9:47

Prayer – Righteous Father, You are good and holy and no evil can be in Your presence. Today I commit all that I am, everything I see, hear and do to be in accordance with Your mission. I will do whatever it takes to follow You. In Jesus' name, Amen.

Day 271

Kingdom Authority and Power

A Truth to Live – The path that leads to God's authority and Kingdom power is narrow, hard and costly, and very few find it. (Matthew 7:13) The best way for me to find this path and not get lost is to follow the same path that Jesus walked when He was on the earth. He came to serve. He befriended sinners. He loved the unlovely and made Himself of no reputation. Wherever He walked people spoke of His authority. When you take Jesus' path, God's authority and Kingdom power will also reign in your life.

Scripture – "*Heal the sick who are there and tell them, 'the Kingdom of God is near you'.*" Luke 10:9

Prayer – Eternal and Wise God, today I choose the narrow road to life. I know that it is not an easy path, but I want to experience the joy and mercy of Your authority. I will empty myself of all ambition and desire so that I can be filled with Your presence and Kingdom Power. In Jesus' name, Amen.

Day 272

Seek Him and Find the Rest

A Truth to Live – God's ways are always true. When I join the mission of God and seek His Kingdom and righteousness He promises that every other need that I have will be met. God has never lied or failed to fulfill His promises.

Scripture – *"Seek His Kingdom and these things will be given to you as well."* Luke 12:31

Prayer – Heavenly Father, today I will seek Your Kingdom and not my own. Help me to find You in every part of my day and to behave humbly and righteously in a way that honors You. I trust that when I put Your Kingdom first, You will take care of all my needs. In Jesus' name, Amen.

Day 273

Finding Greatness in God's Kingdom

A Truth to Live – Earthly power is exercised with might and control, but authority in the Kingdom of God is demonstrated in meekness and humility. I can find true greatness in God's Kingdom when I serve others and stop demanding my rights.

Scripture – *"The kings of the Gentiles lord it over them; but you are not to be like that. Instead, the greatest among you should be like the youngest, and the one who rules like the one who serves. I confer on you a kingdom, just as my Father conferred one on me."* Luke 22:25-29

Prayer – Eternal God, today I will follow Your path of meekness and humility and serve those around me. I know that Your Kingdom is not one of might and control, but of service and sacrificial love. I receive You as the authority in my life and ask that You will confer upon me Your eternal Kingdom. In Jesus' name Amen.

Day 274

The Mission of God Comes First

A Truth to Live – Pressures to conform to the ethics and behaviors of the world can be intense – especially from family, friends and colleagues that I admire. However, joining the mission of God in Kingdom power requires a single loyalty to God above all else.

Scripture – *"No one who has left home or wife or brothers or children for the sake of the Kingdom of God will fail to receive many times as much in this age, and, in the age to come, eternal life."*
Luke 18:29-30

Prayer – Eternal Father, lead me today in Your paths of righteousness for Your name sake. I ask that You would grant me the privilege of journeying with my family and friends in Your Kingdom; but should they choose a different path, then grant me the courage to choose You over the pressures and loyalties of this world. In Jesus' name, Amen.

Day 275

When I Pray

A Truth to Live – I find the most meaning, the greatest passion and lasting purpose in my life when I join the mission of God and live in Kingdom power. It is not an easy path, but it is by far the best. God is ready to release His heavenly power on and through me when I choose Him as my King.

Scripture – *"Jesus said to them, 'When you pray, say: Father hallowed by Your name, Your kingdom come, Your will be done on earth as it is in heaven."* Matthew 6: 9-10

Prayer – Father, I have but one simple prayer for my life, for my family and friends; and for my community, my country and the nations of the earth: Your Kingdom come, Your will be done, on earth as it is in heaven. In Jesus' name, Amen.

Day 276

God Created Me In His Image

A Truth to Live – If I don't know where I'm going, then I'll wind up someplace else. To help me know where to go, when to go and how to get there, I will go to God's Word and meditate on it today and every day.

Scripture – "*So God created man in his own image, in the image of God he created him; male and female he created them.*" Genesis 1:27

Prayer – Heavenly Father, I know that Your Word is more precious than life itself. As I journey through the Bible, help me to read diligently and to learn from You. In Jesus' name, Amen.

Day 277

God’s Covenant is Everlasting

A Truth to Live – To make something my top priority will require me to re-arrange my daily routine. And once I have organized my life around what is most important I will be amazed at how everything falls into place. God made me a priority, creating me in His image and making a covenant with all humankind forever!

Scripture – “*I will establish my covenant as an everlasting covenant between me and you and your descendants after you for the generations to come, to be your God and the God of your descendants after you.* Genesis 17:7

Prayer – Heavenly Father, help me today to see that You have made me Your top priority. You have not only created me, but You have made an everlasting covenant that provides love, forgiveness and the richness of Your presence. Today I choose You. In Jesus’ name, Amen.

Day 278

God Will Never Let Me Go

A Truth to Live – From the beginning of time God has pursued humankind with His love and mercy. His love never ends, and He never tires of pursuing me. As I read God's Word today, I will meditate on God's incredible love for me.

Scripture – *"So Jacob was left alone, and a man wrestled with him till daybreak."* Genesis 32:24

Prayer: Heavenly Father, thank You for the power of Your Word, and the truth that You will never let me go when I trust in You. Grant me the strength today to honor You and to commit my ways to You. In Jesus' name, Amen.

Day 279

God’s Plans Are Good

A Truth to Live – No matter what circumstance I find myself in, it has not escaped the hand or the plan of Almighty God. He is for me and promises to work out my life for the good. The absolute best way to discover His plan is to study God’s Word and apply it to my life.

Harper Lee said, “The book to read is not the one which thinks for you, but the one that makes you think. No book in the world equals the Bible for that."

Scripture –“*You intended to harm me, but God intended it for good to accomplish what is now being done, the saving of many lives.”* Genesis 50:20

Prayer – Gracious Father, thank You for accomplishing good things through my life. Even though others might intend harm for me, You have promised it for good. Thank You. In Jesus’ name, Amen.

Day 280

God Has Created Me For a Purpose

A Truth to Live – God has uniquely and individually shaped me with a purpose that will showcase His glory to the nations of the earth. Far from having a destiny that temporarily satisfies my own desires, God's plan for me brings total fulfillment by connecting me into His broader plan.

Scripture – "*But I have raised you up for this very purpose, that I might show you my power and that my name might be proclaimed in all the earth.*"
Exodus *9:16*

Prayer – Heavenly Father, teach me today as I read Your Word that the reason I exist, the purpose for my life, is much grander than the fleeting contentment of success or being dependent on the affirmation of others. Help me to understand that Your master plan for my life is to show Your power and to proclaim the goodness of Your name throughout the earth. In Jesus' name, Amen.

Day 281

No God But God

A Truth to Live – In today's world people point to many different religions in an effort to find truth, hope and eternal life. But only one true God offers complete and total forgiveness through a gift of love. It is God's passion to be reconciled back to humankind, and He restored this broken path by offering His only Son for my salvation. As I receive Him I am granted eternal life and as I follow His Word God promises the blessings of His presence.

Scripture – *"You shall have no other gods before me."* Exodus 20:3

Prayer – Eternal and Righteous God, thank You for Your unending mercy and patience. You loved me before I knew You, and You have charted out the course for me to follow that will align my life with You and the blessings that are awaiting me. Help me today to be diligent to read Your Word and to plant it in my heart. In Jesus' name, Amen.

Day 282

God Makes His Way Abundantly Clear

A Truth to Live – God is not secretive. He has no special or hidden code to decipher, no complex set of rituals to perform. His purpose and His will are true, simple and self-evident. He wants to be reconciled to me. He loves me and has made a way for me to come back to Him through His Son Jesus Christ.

Scripture – "*In all the travels of the Israelites, whenever the cloud lifted from above the tabernacle, they would set out; but if the cloud did not lift, they did not set out - until the day it lifted.*" Exodus 40:36-37

Prayer – Heavenly Father, thank You for making Your ways evident, for not hiding behind mindless rituals or meaningless repetition. Help me to focus on You, Your love and Your purpose in my life today. In Jesus' name, Amen.

Day 283

God Desires to Speak to Me

A Truth to Live – God is a communicator. He loves me with an ever-lasting love and always takes the initiative to seek me out, to show His love and to demonstrate His compassion toward me. My role is to simply wait, listen and to respond to the powerful truth of His Word.

Scripture – "*The Lord called to Moses and spoke to him from the Tent of Meeting.*" Leviticus 1:1

Prayer – Gracious, Eternal and Powerful Father, Yours alone is the kingdom and the power and might and authority – in this age, on this earth and in the age to come. Thank You for reaching down to love me and to speak loving words to my heart. I will respond to You today and serve You with all my heart. In Jesus' name, Amen.

Day 284

God's Goodness Never Changes

A Truth to Live – Our world is changing so rapidly that sometimes it seems that nothing ever stays the same. In the last few years alone I have seen massive improvements in technology and infrastructure, but also, in many cases, the disintegration of the family unit. However, there is one thing that will never change: GOD. He is righteous, pure, loving and holy – forever.

Scripture – "*Be holy because I, the Lord your God, am holy.*" Leviticus 19:2

Prayer – Heavenly Father, thank You for being consistent and never changing. You are righteous, holy and pure and Your mercy toward me never fails. Help me today to measure and align my own life to You so that I can dwell in Your presence. In Jesus' name, Amen.

Day 285

It's About Him

A Truth to Live – Though there are many competing voices in my world that vie for my attention, my time and my resources, there is just one voice that is worth listening to; one person worth following and one God worth serving. Reading His Word is the best way to understand Him and His ways.

Scripture – *"The LORD bless you and keep you; the LORD make his face shine upon you and be gracious to you; the LORD turn his face toward you and give you peace."* Numbers 6:24-26

Prayer – Gracious Father, I ask today that You would turn Your attention toward me and bless me with Your love, mercy and peace. In Jesus' name, Amen.

Day 286

God has Good Things in Store

A Truth to Live – Since God is in charge of my day, my circumstances, my community and even the nations of the world – He can be trusted. Even when circumstances look evil, or times are difficult God is the One who promises to bring His goodness to light in every situation.

My response to God's interaction helps to determine my involvement in His grand plan. As I read the Bible I know I am not going to like everything I read in the Bible. When I come across disagreeable portions, I will allow myself to be amazed instead of appalled; struggle rather than disengage. This is all part of the experience. I will trust that much will become apparent as I continue my reading.

Scripture – "*Now the people complained about their hardships in the hearing of the Lord, and when he heard them his anger was aroused.*" Numbers 11:1

Prayer – God of Mercy, I thank You today that You are in charge, that You have my best interest in mind, and that You love me with an everlasting love. Help me to view my world and my circumstances through the lens of Your wisdom and not through the limitations of my own experiences. In Jesus' name, Amen.

Day 287

God Always Keeps His Word

A Truth to Live – God never violates His character nor breaks His Word. He is completely dependable, always trustworthy and always acts for my good. In the covenant relationship that God has established with those who follow Him, He expects the same – a consistent honorable upholding of my words and commitment to Him.

Scripture – "*Moses said to the heads of the tribes of Israel: "This is what the LORD commands: When a man makes a vow to the LORD or takes an oath to obligate himself by a pledge, he must not break his word but must do everything he said.*"
Numbers 30:1-2

Prayer – Gracious Father, thank You for the gift I hold in my hands. May Your Spirit fill me and interpret Your precious words for me as I read them. In Your Son's name I pray, Amen.

Day 288

God Deserves My Utmost

A Truth to Live – God deserves nothing less than my best. Think of it this way. Since God created me, knows what is best for me, has charted a path for me that is filled with the abundance of His presence and has provided both a standard to live by and forgiveness for my shortcomings, He is worthy of my very best.

Scripture – "*Love the LORD your God with all your heart and with all your soul and with all your strength.* Deuteronomy 6:5

Prayer – Heavenly Father, I know that You have provided for me the path of success and a journey map to get there. Help me to find the strength and the time to study Your Word and Your ways so that I can devote all of me to following You. In Jesus' name, Amen.

Day 289

God Has Paved a Way for My Success

A Truth to Live – Many people wonder what their next steps should be, or how they should respond to certain options that arise in the course of life. God's solution to these moments of uncertainty has been charted out in His Word, and it begins with radical obedience and reverence. The more I study His Word and focus on His greatness the easier it is to follow His path to success.

Helen Keller said: "Unless we form the habit of going to the Bible in bright moments as well as in trouble, we cannot fully respond to its consolations because we lack equilibrium between light and darkness."

Scripture – "*Observe the commands of the Lord your God, walking in his ways and revering him.*" Deuteronomy 8:6

Prayer – All knowing Father, today I turn the attention of my mind and heart away from my own understanding and toward Your infinite wisdom and gentle leading. I commit that You will be my guide and that I will walk in Your ways, honoring You with the words that I speak and the meditations of my heart. In Jesus' name, Amen.

Day 290

God's Word is Faithful and True

A Truth to Live – God is consistently and constantly committed to the fulfillment of His Word. From the moment I wake up until the moment I sleep – and while I am asleep – God's Word is at work to help me find Him and His ways. While it is true that there are consequences to pay when I choose to stray from His guidance, it is also true that His rewards are equally real.

Scripture – "*Then the LORD said to him, 'This is the land I promised on oath to Abraham, Isaac and Jacob when I said, 'I will give it to your descendants.' I have let you see it with your eyes, but you will not cross over into it'.*" Deuteronomy 34:4

Prayer – Eternal God, help me today to choose the right path by following You. There are many temptations and distractions that come my way, and I can be easily turned away from what I know is best. I am asking for Your Spirit to lead and guide me into all truth; and to the blessings that You have for me. In Jesus' name, Amen.

Day 291

God is Always With Me

A Truth to Live – There is nothing, absolutely nothing that can separate me from the love of God. And I choose to follow Him, it gets even better. He promises to be with me in every conversation, conflict or circumstance – leading and guiding me each step of the way.

Scripture – "*Have I not commanded you? Be strong and courageous. Do not be terrified; do not be discouraged, for the LORD your God will be with you wherever you go.*" Joshua 1:9

Prayer – Eternal and Almighty God, thank You for encouraging me to be strong and courageous each step of my day. I will choose to have faith in You and not live in fear or become discouraged because I know that You will be with me wherever I go. In Jesus' name, Amen.

Day 292

God Wants Me to Serve Him

A Truth to Live – Every day I make choices. Some are good and, realistically, some are not so good. But there is one fundamental choice that God asks me to make. It is about the big picture and the small details and begins with a commitment to God and His way of life.

Scripture – "*But if serving the LORD seems undesirable to you, then choose for yourselves this day whom you will serve, whether the gods your forefathers served beyond the River, or the gods of the Amorites, in whose land you are living. But as for me and my household, we will serve the LORD.*"
Joshua 24:15

Prayer – Heavenly Father, I choose You today. Help me to commit to thinking Your thoughts, walking according to Your path and living according to Your Word. Give me the courage to choose You and to lead my family to You. In Jesus' name, Amen.

Day 293

God Wants to be in Charge

A Truth to Live – When I take the leadership responsibility of my own life there is a very good chance that I will meet a dead end, be overcome by discouragement or be trapped in spiritual darkness. But, when God is in charge everything works. Confusion leaves, distractions fade away, temptations become smaller and the future becomes clearer.

Scripture – "*But Gideon told them, "I will not rule over you, nor will my son rule over you. The LORD will rule over you."* Judges 8:23

Prayer – Heavenly Father, today I thank You for leading and guiding me by the power of Your Spirit. Today I expect that my issues, confusion and despair will fade away and will be replaced by Your goodness and truth. In Jesus' name, Amen.

Day 294

God is God

A Truth to Live – When the truth of God and His mercy begins to renew my mind and re-shape my actions, my friendships will change. While God will give me the strength to continue to share His Good News with those in need, He will also surround me with a new and stronger set of friends who will build me up in my faith.

Scripture – "*But Ruth replied, "Don't urge me to leave you or to turn back from you. Where you go I will go, and where you stay I will stay. Your people will be my people and your God my God. Where you die I will die, and there I will be buried. May the LORD deal with me, be it ever so severely, if anything but death separates you and me."* Ruth 1:16-17

Prayer – Mighty God, You are the Eternal King and no one will ever over throw You from the throne of Heaven. Thank you for transforming my heart, renewing my mind re-shaping my actions and re-building friendships in my life that are true and help me to increase my faith in You. In Jesus' name, Amen.

Day 295

God is Waiting to Hear from Me

A Truth to Live – God has ears to hear, the time to listen, and the right answer to every question I could possibly ask Him. He is waiting for me to stop looking for answers from within my own strength or seeking others out for their counsel. He is the source of all knowledge and wisdom, and He desires to teach me the way that is good and right.

Scripture – "*As for me, far be it from me that I should sin against the LORD by failing to pray for you. And I will teach you the way that is good and right.*"
1 Samuel 12:23

Prayer – Heavenly Father, today I make the wise choice to turn to You for the answers to all my questions, concerns and difficulties. You are the way, the truth and the life, and I trust in You to help me do the right thing today and follow the right path in the future. In Jesus' name, Amen.

Day 296

God Looks at the Heart

A Truth to Live – First impressions are made very quickly. Within seconds I can make far-reaching conclusions based on a handshake, a smile, clothes or comments. God, however, views people very differently. He is not impressed by outward appearances but rather on people's inner thoughts and behaviors.

Scripture – "*But the LORD said to Samuel, "Do not consider his appearance or his height, for I have rejected him. The LORD does not look at the things man looks at. Man looks at the outward appearance, but the LORD looks at the heart."* 1 Samuel 16:7

Prayer – Gracious Heavenly Father, thank You for choosing me, for loving me and providing salvation through the work of Your Son on the cross. Since You look at the heart and are moved by love, help me today to not draw wrong conclusions based on outwardly focused first impressions but instead to be moved by Your love and compassion for others. In Jesus' name, Amen.

Day 297

God Makes the Final Choice

A Truth to Live – While the world chooses its leaders based on popularity, looks, wealth or influence God chooses leaders for His Kingdom work on one simple criteria: the heart. Finding my way into God's favor begins with a commitment to honor Him, to have reverence for Him and to live in radical obedience.

Scripture – "*But the LORD said to Samuel, "Do not consider his appearance or his height, for I have rejected him. The LORD does not look at the things man looks at. Man looks at the outward appearance, but the LORD looks at the heart.*" 1 Samuel 16:7

Prayer – Eternally Wise God, help me today to focus on the core of who I really am. It is not the clothes I wear or even the conversations that I have with others. What really matters is the simplicity, purity and focused direction of my heart. Help me to choose You. In Jesus' name, Amen.

Day 298

God's Love is True and Never-Ending

A Truth to Live – The news is filled with short-term romances, selfishly focused passion and "love" that seeks its own benefit. Nothing could be further from a God-formed love. God's love always seeks the benefit of others, is eternal and has at its core truth and mercy.

Scripture – "*The king was shaken. He went up to the room over the gateway and wept. As he went, he said: "O my son Absalom! My son, my son Absalom! If only I had died instead of you-O Absalom, my son, my son!"* 2 Samuel 18:33

Prayer – Loving Father, help me today to focus on You, the source of true love, mercy and forgiveness. I am tired of being hurt by the selfish motives of others and admit to You that I have been no better. I have chosen to love conditionally. But from today onward I want Your gracious, self-less love to fill my being and over flow into the lives of others. In Jesus' name, Amen.

Day 299

God Wants Me to Prosper

A Truth to Live – There are lots of self-help books, CDs and other tools that are produced each year to motivate people to success. Then there is the revelation found in God's Word. God's plans for me are good, strong and faith-filled with a big desire for me to succeed. But God's ways begin with a radical obedience to His Word and an honoring of Him above else.

Scripture – "*When the time drew near for David to die, he gave a charge to Solomon his son, 'I am about to go the way of all the earth,' he said. 'So be strong, show yourself a man, and observe what the LORD your God requires: Walk in his ways, and keep his decrees and commands, his laws and requirements, as written in the Law of Moses, so that you may prosper in all you do and wherever you go'....*" 1 Kings 2:1-3

Prayer – Eternal Father, thank You for wanting the best for me. I am choosing today to no longer follow shortsighted advice that has me look inside myself for answers. Instead, I will look to You and will keep Your commands. In Jesus' name, Amen.

Day 300

God Deserves the Best

A Truth to Live – Most of my daily routines are filled with busyness; chores to accomplish, duties to fulfill and mundane activities that, to some, don't deserve my best. In every situation, God deserves my very best efforts, especially when it comes creating a place for Him to dwell.

Scripture – "*In the eleventh year in the month of Bul, the eighth month, the temple was finished in all its details according to its specifications. He had spent seven years building it. It took Solomon thirteen years, however, to complete the construction of his palace.*" 1 Kings 6:38-1 Kings 7:1

Prayer – Heavenly Father, I honor You today. Help me to see You and Your Word as my top priority! No matter how long it takes, or how much effort it takes I want my life to reflect Your saving grace and the truth of Your Word. In Jesus' name, Amen.

Day 301

God Speaks Louder When it is Silent

A Truth to Live – Most of my life is filled with noise. Radios, TV, music and conversations fill the "space" of my mind and compete for my attention. But the voice of God will not compete as an equal with any other input. When I learn to quiet my soul and reduce the noise around me there is usually a still small whisper of truth.

Scripture – "*The LORD said, "Go out and stand on the mountain in the presence of the LORD, for the LORD is about to pass by. Then a great and powerful wind tore the mountains apart and shattered the rocks before the LORD, but the LORD was not in the wind.*

After the wind there was an earthquake, but the LORD was not in the earthquake. After the earthquake came a fire, but the LORD was not in the fire. And after the fire came a gentle whisper. When Elijah heard it, he pulled his cloak over his face and went out and stood at the mouth of the cave." 1 Kings 19:11-13a

Prayer – Gracious Father, I thank You today for Your patience and mercy. Help me today to tune my ears away from the noise and interruptions of my day and find "space" to be still, to be quiet and to listen to the powerful truth and obedience of Your Word. In Jesus' name, Amen.

Day 302

God is a Healer

A Truth to Live – Life is filled with ups and downs, pleasantries and dangers, the routine and the unexpected. Each day is filled with a combination of circumstances that cause stress and peace. I can learn to navigate through the obstacles of life when I make God and His eternal word the #1 priority in my life. He not only has a solution – He is the solution to my needs.

Scripture – "*The stew was poured out for the men, but as they began to eat it, they cried out, 'O man of God, there is death in the pot!' And they could not eat it. Elisha said, 'Get some flour.' He put it into the pot and said, 'Serve it to the people to eat.' And there was nothing harmful in the pot.*" 2 Kings 4:40-41.

Prayer – Eternal Father, there is so much about my day of which I have no control. Rather than view these unexpected events as things that add stress to me, today I am asking You to help me yield each one of them to You. As I apply the truth of Your Word to my day, I thank You that Your peace will dominate my day. In Jesus' name, Amen.

Day 303

God Can Be Trusted

A Truth to Live – Which of the news reports, documentaries and commentaries are true and objective? Truthfully every report given by a person is limited and biased to their education and experience. How much better it is to receive the report of the Lord – it is also accurate, truthful and filled with love and mercy.

By reading ALL of God's Word, I am learning much more about Him than if I just read bits and pieces of the Bible. Ideally, this learning will be a springboard to a new way of relating to Him.

Scripture – "*Hezekiah trusted in the LORD, the God of Israel. There was no one like him among all the kings of Judah, either before him or after him.*" 2 Kings 18:5

Prayer – Eternal Savior and Mighty God, thank You for being the Way, the Truth and the Life. When my world seems filled with confusion help me to always turn to You. You are my light and my salvation. In Jesus' name, Amen.

Day 304

God Desires to Bless Me!

A Truth to Live – God has chosen to declare His goodness and glory in the earth through those who choose to follow Him. This means that if I choose Him to be my Savior and Guide, He will expand His influence in my life. He will use me in ever increasing measure.

Scripture – "*Jabez was more honorable than his brothers. His mother had named him Jabez, saying, 'I gave birth to him in pain.' Jabez cried out to the God of Israel, 'Oh, that you would bless me and enlarge my territory! Let your hand be with me, and keep me from harm so that I will be free from pain.' And God granted his request." 1 Chronicles 4:9-10*

Prayer – Merciful Father, I am thankful today that You have chosen to declare Your glory among the nations and to reconcile all people back to You through people like me. Transform me so that I can be used to a greater degree to share Your goodness with others. In Jesus' name, Amen.

Day 305

God is Worthy

A Truth to Live – There is only one supernatural being who is worth emulating, following and living for. He is good, noble, righteous, holy, pure, filled with love and peace, slow to anger, quick to forgive and always willing to reconcile Himself to those who choose to follow Him. He is God, and He is worthy of my worship, trustable with my soul, and devoted to my eternal well-being.

Scripture – "*Give thanks to the LORD, call on his name; make known among the nations what he has done.* 1 Chronicles 16:8

Prayer – Heavenly Father, I choose to worship You today. There is no other person on earth or in heaven that is worthy like You. I know that when You are in the right place in my own heart I am at peace so I ask You to reign in me. In Jesus' name, Amen.

Day 306

God Exalts the Humble

A Truth to Live – Many people seek to fill a void in their heart by spending enormous amounts of energy promoting their achievements, ideas, and opinions. This "me first" attitude can create moments of satisfaction but they are short-lived. God's way is better. He seeks out those whose hearts are humble, moldable and focused on Him and then blesses them.

Scripture – *"The LORD highly exalted Solomon in the sight of all Israel and bestowed on him royal splendor such as no king over Israel ever had before."*
1 Chronicles 29:25

Prayer – Heavenly Father, help me to understand that the way to find peace and contentment in my own life comes through humbly submitting all that I am to Your bountiful hand and loving heart. You have a future for me that is good and filled with hope, and today I exchange my broken ideals with Your grand plans. In Jesus' name, Amen.

Day 307

God Never Changes

A Truth to Live – When God made a covenant promise with humankind it was made to last forever. Unlike so many of the conditional promises of today, God's oath was simple: His presence and provision would be the reward for those who follow Him. This means that to qualify for His blessings, all I need to do is follow His Son, Jesus!

Scripture – *"As for us, the Lord is our God, and we have not forsaken Him."* 2 Chronicles 13:10

Prayer – Gracious and Never Changing God, how I praise You today for Your faithfulness. Your love and mercy never cease, and Your Word is life-giving to my soul. I commit to honor my commitment to Your covenant promise and look forward to the blessings of Your presence and provision. In Jesus' name, Amen.

Day 308

God Honors His Word

A Truth to Live – Since God can always be trusted to fulfill His promises, I am safe to stretch my faith in His direction. He hears my heart cries and will respond to my needs. As my Heavenly Father, He is watching over me and caring for my needs. He is good, and He wants to share His goodness with me.

Scripture – *"Hezekiah…did right in the eyes of the Lord, just as his father David had done."*
2 Chronicles 29:1-2

Prayer – Eternal Father, You are trustworthy and full of honor and integrity. Even when the world around me is filled with compromise and changing opinion I can count on Your Word to be true, faithful and for my good. Help me to remember to put You first today. In Jesus' name, Amen.

Day 309

God's Love Lasts Forever

A Truth to Live – The love and affection of those around me doesn't always last. In fact, often times it is not even predictably consistent. But the Creator God is different. His love for me will last for eternity, and His plans for me are for my benefit. When I respond to His love, He will never neglect or ignore me. That is the truth of His Word.

Scripture – *"With praise and thanksgiving they sang to the LORD: 'He is good; his love to Israel endures forever.' And all the people gave a great shout of praise to the LORD, because the foundation of the house of the LORD was laid."* Ezra 3:11

Prayer – Loving Heavenly Father, today I am turning to You to find the affirmation and affection that I need. Help me to stop turning toward others to meet the needs that only You can fill. As I study Your Word today help me to give praise, to offer thanks and to exclaim my love for You. In Jesus' name, Amen.

Day 310

God is Strength

A Truth to Live – Discouragement, despair and loneliness are three weapons that the enemy uses to drain me of emotional energy and strength. But God has provided just the right tool guaranteed to destroy this work of the Devil – it is joy in God and His goodness. When I apply joy to my life sorrow, mourning and sadness disappear!

Scripture – "*Nehemiah said, 'Go and enjoy choice food and sweet drinks, and send some to those who have nothing prepared. This day is sacred to our Lord. Do not grieve, for the joy of the LORD is your strength'.*" Nehemiah 8:10

Prayer – Everlasting God, today I will reject the sadness and loneliness that often come when I think of the circumstances and responsibilities before me. In their place I will place my hope in You and will recount with joy all of amazing work You have done. The joy of the Lord is my strength. In Jesus' name, Amen.

Day 311

God Has a Divine Plan for Me

A Truth to Live – There is a reason for my existence. It is much more than running errands, doing chores and earning a living. God has created me with a divine purpose, a real destiny and gives me a passion to fulfill His plan. I was made for the moment!

Scripture – "*When Esther's words were reported to Mordecai, he sent back this answer: 'Do not think that because you are in the king's house you alone of all the Jews will escape. For if you remain silent at this time, relief and deliverance for the Jews will arise from another place, but you and your father's family will perish. And who knows but that you have come to royal position for such a time as this?'*

Then Esther sent this reply to Mordecai: 'Go, gather together all the Jews who are in Susa, and fast for me. Do not eat or drink for three days, night or day. I and my maids will fast as you do. When this is done, I will go to the king, even though it is against the law. And if I perish, I perish'." Esther 4:12-16

Prayer – Heavenly Father, my heart is filled with expectation and hope today as I focus on the reality that You created me for a purpose. I am more than an accident, or a collision of atoms randomly appearing in time. You have orchestrated history so that my contribution will give You glory and spread Your fame in the earth. Thank You. In Jesus' name, Amen.

Day 312

God Restores

A Truth to Live – God is near and not distant. He sees what is going on around me, hears my prayers and is moved by the cry of my heart. He will never reject me or strengthen those who oppose me. He is God and He is good. I will trust God to fill me with hope and joy.

Scripture – "*Surely God does not reject a blameless man or strengthen the hands of evildoers. He will yet fill your mouth with laughter and your lips with shouts of joy. Your enemies will be clothed in shame, and the tents of the wicked will be no more.*" Job 8:20-22

Prayer – Eternal God, how grateful I am today that You are not a distant unreachable God. You hear my cries, see my pain and desire to bring wholeness to my life. I pray today that I will learn to focus on Your eternal goodness and not the temporary troubles around me. In Jesus' name, Amen.

Day 313

God Owns it All

A Truth to Live – God is the owner of everything and is the originator of all that is good, pleasant and filled with peace. When the resources of this world are used for selfish gain or privilege God is being robbed, and His intention to bless others is being perverted.

The best way to keep my way pure and my motives right is to make a habit of reading God's Word each and every day. John Quincy Adams said: "My custom is to read four or five chapters of the Bible every morning immediately after rising... It seems to me the most suitable manner of beginning the day... It is an invaluable and inexhaustible mine of knowledge and virtue."

Scripture – "*"Everything under heaven belongs to me."* Job 41:11

Prayer – Heavenly Father, You are the eternal Creator and the One who holds the earth together. Help me today to learn from You and to live in reverence for all that You are and all that You have. I commit today to honor and care for Your world. In Jesus' name, Amen.

Day 314

God Gives

A Truth to Live – Most people with power always demand more of my time, my finances, my allegiance and future. But God is different. He is a giving God. He gives love, forgiveness, strength, mercy, kindness, and responsibility all in an effort to make His name known so that I might enjoy life the way it was meant to be!

Scripture – "*Ask of me and I will give you the nations as your inheritance, the ends of the earth your possession.*" Psalms 2:8

Prayer – Righteous and Holy Father, I am so honored and blessed today to be considered by You as Your child. Thank You for sending Jesus, Your Son, to die on the cross for me and to extend to me the promises of Abraham. Help me to walk in obedience and to enjoy the bounty of Your love and provision. In Jesus' name, Amen.

Day 315

God is a Deliverer

A Truth to Live – When I am in deep trouble, or facing a crisis beyond my own ability to solve, there is just One who can rescue from disaster. He is God. Since my Savior is good and filled with loving compassion He desires to help me in times of need and to bring me into a better place.

Scripture – "*Blessed is he who has regard for the weak; the LORD delivers him in times of trouble.* Psalms 41:1

Prayer – Eternal God, thank You for being the great Rescuer. I thank You for finding me and delivering me out of the pit of darkness, wrong-doing and selfish living. My empty life has been transformed by the power of Your Name! In Jesus' name, Amen.

Day 316

God Fulfills His Purpose for Me

A Truth to Live – Many people mistakenly believe that God is passive, distant and not actively involved in the affairs of humankind. Nothing could be further from the truth. God has been creating since the moment the earth began, and He is working today to make sure His good plans for me come to pass. He is for me!

Scripture – *"I cry out to God Most High, to God, who fulfills His purpose for me."* Psalms 57:2

Prayer – Gracious and Loving God, You are ever kind and loving. Before I awakened today You were already charting a course for me that is good and filled with love and mercy. Thank You for being the One who plans out and fulfills Your purpose for me. In Jesus' name, Amen.

Day 317

God Loves

A Truth to Live – God is slow to anger but abounds in goodness, kindness and favor. Like a loving and caring Father, He desires nothing but the best for His children. Unlike other religious deities God is for me not against me; and He is faithful to His Word and to me. I will ask Him today to show me His way and His path for me.

Scripture – "*But you, O Lord, are a compassionate and gracious God, slow to anger, abounding in love and faithfulness.*" Psalm 86:15

Prayer – Gracious Father, thank You for being compassionate and understanding. You see the moments when I falter or stray from the path that is best for me, and Your love brings me back to the place that I should be. Help me today to stay in Your love and mercy by making right choices and responding with my heart to You. In Jesus' name, Amen.

Day 318

God Deserves Praise

A Truth to Live – Everything that lives is fueled by energy. People need calories, cars require gasoline, lights need electricity and God's creation is fueled by praise. Far from being an egocentric demand, God's call for worship and praise is the single act that puts life back into proper perspective and creates order in our complex world.

Scripture – *"Shout for joy to the LORD, all the earth. Worship the LORD with gladness; come before him with joyful songs."* Psalm 100:1-2

Prayer – Heavenly Father, You deserve the praise and honor of my heart. When I look at the complexity of the human body, the order of the universe or the tenderness of my own heart I am amazed at Your handiwork. Help me to remember to give You the honor that is due to You today. In Jesus' name, Amen.

Day 319

God Has Plans for My Good

A Truth to Live – God's plan for my life is good. Contrary to many who offer short-term quick fixes, solutions for happy thoughts and a better life, God's ways are always good, they always last and they never fade. Finding the truth about Him and life in God's Word is the sure way to keep me walking strong and filled with hope.

Scripture – "*I have hidden your word in my heart that I might not sin against you.*" Psalm 119:11

Prayer – Righteous and Wise God, thank You for the treasure of Your Word. I know that by reading, meditating and following Your truths I will find peace in my heart, direction for my day and hope for the future. Help me to be faithful to place Your truth in my heart. In Jesus' name, Amen.

Day 320

God Gives Eternal Hope

A Truth to Live – Sometimes, my emotions can be wounded more easily and even quicker than my body. But I can reduce the damaging power of negative and hurtful words by turning the attention of my mind and heart to the wisdom and truth of God's Word. God has designed His Word to be my greatest protection from pain.

Scripture – *"Above all else guard your heart, for it is the wellspring of life."* Proverbs 4:23

Prayer – Eternal God, I thank You today for the power and truth of Your Word. It is my source of strength, my daily guide and the revealer of truth. Thank You. Help me today to guard my heart with Your truth so that my heart will be life-giving and a blessing to those around me. In Jesus' name, Amen.

Day 321

God Knows the Way

A Truth to Live – Have a question? God has the answer. Confused? God has the wisdom. Feeling lonely or in despair? He is peace. Lost? God knows the way. In a world that over shares and is more concerned with an immediate response than a correct solution – God is ever wise, and His Word is always true.

Scripture – *"There is a way that seems right to a man, but in the end it leads to death."* Proverbs 14:12

Prayer – Eternal Wise God, I come to You today grateful for Your eternal wisdom and Your gentle patience. Help me to listen attentively to the truth of Your Word and to walk in Your life-giving ways. In Jesus' name, Amen.

Day 322

God Measures My Actions

A Truth to Live – My world measures, evaluates and even memorizes the words of others to gain a sense of who they are and where they might be headed. But God is different. While words are important in understanding a person's motives, God observes and measures me by my actions.

Scripture – *"Even a child is known by his actions, by whether his conduct is pure and right."*
Proverbs 20:11

Prayer – Heavenly Father, thank You for being my truth and my guide. When I travel through difficult moments or awaken to a beautiful day You are always there. Help me today to prioritize my actions as the true signal of my heart and devotion to You. In Jesus' name, Amen.

Day 323

God Has a Time for Everything

A Truth to Live – God was, He is, and He will be. This means that before anything began God pre-existed. He is ever-present now and will be here forever. Because He created the earth and all that is in it I can trust Him in every season of life, knowing that he will be with me.

Scripture – "*There is a time for everything, and a season for every activity under heaven: a time to be born and a time to die, a time to plant and a time to uproot, a time to kill and a time to heal, a time to tear down and a time to build, a time to weep and a time to laugh, a time to mourn and a time to dance, a time to scatter stones and a time to gather them, a time to embrace and a time to refrain, a time to search and a time to give up, a time to keep and a time to throw away, a time to tear and a time to mend, a time to be silent and a time to speak, a time to love and a time to hate, a time for war and a time for peace.*" Ecclesiastes 3:1-8

Prayer – Heavenly Father, thank You for being in charge, responsible and confident about the world You have made. I come to You today knowing my own shortcomings and asking for Your wisdom to get through this "season" and to glorify You in all that I do. In Jesus' name, Amen.

Day 324

God's is Wise

A Truth to Live – I have no lack for access to information. I can learn from peers, mentors, parents, books, newspapers, television, magazines and the internet. But where can I find truth in the midst of all this knowledge? Real wisdom and understanding come from God and His Word.

Scripture – "*Hear, O heavens! Listen, O earth! For the LORD has spoken: 'I reared children and brought them up, but they have rebelled against me. The ox knows his master, the donkey his owner's manger, but Israel does not know, my people do not understand'.*" Isaiah 1:2-3

Prayer – Heavenly Father, today I make the choice to follow the wisdom of Your words and to align my life to Your ways. Help me to prioritize my time to seek You in every situation and to order my days according to the truth of Your Word. In Jesus' name, Amen.

Day 325

God is My Anchor

A Truth to Live – God is always there. He is an anchor that enables me to weather the most difficult storms and a rock of strength providing me a firm grip when everything else around me fails. When I choose Him, I am placing my life in safe, strong and capable hands.

Scripture – "*The LORD will have compassion on Jacob; once again he will choose Israel and will settle them in their own land. Aliens will join them and unite with the house of Jacob.*" Isaiah 14:1

Prayer – Heavenly Father, You are my Rock and my Strength – always present in times of trouble. Help me to adjust my focus away from the storms that come and go and instead place my attention and devotion on You. You will rescue me! In Jesus' name, Amen.

Day 326

God's Word Stands Forever

A Truth to Live – God is ever trustworthy and His character is consistent and wholly good. Even the thoughts and opinions of those around me may shift, change or even contradict one another, I can count on God's Word to be filled with His mercy, righteousness and justice.

Scripture – "*The grass withers and the flowers fail, but the word of our God stands forever.*" Isaiah 40:8

Prayer – Heavenly Father, I am grateful today that Your Word is true, everlasting, and consistent with Your character. You never change and You are ever at work to fulfill the words of Scripture in our world. Help me today to focus on Your work in my world and not to be distracted by the short-lived opinions of those around me. In Jesus' name, Amen.

Day 327

There is One God

A Truth to Live – I live in an age of pluralism where all things are leveled to be equal. But God is not one among many gods from which to choose. He is the only one true and living God. As the Creator, Sustainer and Redeemer of my world God alone is the One who can speak life into any situation.

Scripture – "*Turn to me and be saved, all you ends of the earth; for I am God, and there is no other.*" Isaiah 45:22

Prayer – Heavenly Father, I am grateful today that You alone are God. You were before all things began, You are and You will be. There is no competition or challenge to Your sovereignty or power. Yet You choose to love and redeem those who willingly receive the gift of Your Son. Help me today to be a true follower of You. In Jesus' name, Amen.

Day 328

God's Word Always Accomplishes Its Purpose

A Truth to Live – God's Word is true, active and is always at work to accomplish its purposes. There is not one promise, decree or warning in Scripture that can be limited or thwarted by another power. Since there is no other God, His Word is supreme.

Scripture – "*As the rain and the snow come down from heaven, and do not return to it without watering the earth and making it bud and flourish, so that it yields seed for the sower and bread for the eater, so is my word that goes out from my mouth: It will not return to me empty, but will accomplish what I desire and achieve the purpose for which I sent it.*"
Isaiah 55:10-11

Prayer – Eternal God, I am thankful today that Your words are true and never change! Because I have submitted my life to You and received Your Son Jesus into my life, Your Word is at work in me! I am so grateful that You are patient and kind and working in my life so that I can be conformed more each day into Your image. In Jesus' name, Amen.

Day 329

God has a Destiny for Me

A Truth to Live – I am not here by chance or the product of a coincidence. God formed me, designed me, and has something uniquely good for me to do while I am here on this earth. I will never allow any other message to be true in my life – God loves me, and He has incredible plans for my life.

Scripture – "*Before I formed you in the womb I knew you, before you were born I set you apart; I appointed you as a prophet to the nations.*" Jeremiah 1:5

Prayer – Eternal and Ever Powerful God, thank You for loving me and creating me uniquely to accomplish something for You on this earth. Many of those around me live in despair because they have been taught that fate has pre-determined their days. Or even worse, that there is no meaning for their lives. Help me, God to live in the truth of Your Word and to remember today that You have set me apart to glorify You. In Jesus' name, Amen.

Day 330

There is No One Like Our God

A Truth to Live – The world is full of man-made idols and ideologies that cripple my thoughts and deaden my heart. But God is both life giving and lives forevermore. When I pray, He listens because He is there to love and guide me toward all truth and love. He alone is God.

Scripture – "*Who should not revere you, O King of the nations? This is your due. Among all the wise men of the nations and in all their kingdoms, there is no one like you. They are all senseless and foolish; they are taught by worthless wooden idols.*"
Jeremiah 10:7-8

Prayer – Holy and Eternal God, today I place my complete allegiance and commitment to You. I will no longer follow any idols or ideologies that come between me and You, or the truth of Your Word. Help me to remain faithful to You and to share Your goodness with others. In Jesus' name, Amen.

Day 331

God's Word Has Power

A Truth to Live – There are many promises made every day by well-intentioned people. Some of their words will come to pass and some will not. But the words of the Eternal God have infinite power, will never fail and are always at work to accomplish His mission.

Scripture – "'Let *the prophet who has a dream tell his dream, but let the one who has my word speak it faithfully. For what has straw to do with grain?' declares the LORD. 'Is not my word like fire,' declares the LORD, 'and like a hammer that breaks a rock in pieces?'"* Jeremiah 23:28-29

Prayer – Eternal God, I am thankful that Your Word is true - always true and never failing. What You promise will come to pass and what You decree will be. I humble myself today under the authority of Your loving Son and the power of Your Word. Help me to be obedient as I grow in my relationship with You. In Jesus' name, Amen.

Day 332

God Answers

A Truth to Live – The twists and turns of life often bring surprising questions to my mind. Too often I attempt to solve these riddles of life on my own instead of turning to the one who created life itself. The best way forward is to call on God, because He promised to hear attentively and to respond to my need.

Scripture – *"Call to me and I will answer you and tell you great and unsearchable things you do not know."* Jeremiah 33:3

Prayer – Gracious Father, thank You for being alive and attentive to my needs. I admit to You that sometimes it is difficult for me to realize that You always desire good for me. Today I will call to You and then expect Your revelation to make sense of my today and my tomorrow. In Jesus' name, Amen.

Day 333

By God's Grace

A Truth to Live – Many believe that by their own strength they can muster the courage and strength to withstand the storms of life and navigate well. But actually the opposite is true. Left to myself I am always lost, my heart is broken, and my destiny shattered. But God's grace enables me to find Him and to follow His path toward a life that is holy and pure.

Scripture – "*How deserted lies the city, once so full of people! How like a widow is she, who once was great among the nations! She who was queen among the provinces has now become a slave.*" Lamentations 1:1

Prayer – Gracious Father, today I choose to receive Your grace and acknowledge that You alone are my King and my God. I will follow You alone and look to You as my source of direction, guidance and comfort. Thank You for being with me in every situation! In Jesus' name, Amen.

Day 334

God Reigns

A Truth to Live – God reigns. Today, tomorrow and forever. He has always been in charge and always will be. He is not threatened by the words of men and their gods. He alone reigns forever and ever. How awesome it is that the God who reigns chooses to love and cherish me!

Scripture – "*You, O LORD, reign forever; your throne endures from generation to generation.*" Lamentations 5:19

Prayer – Heavenly Father, You reign! Today, tomorrow and forever. I rest in You knowing that Your words are true, Your wisdom is right and Your kindness is just. Teach me today to live with the mercy You give and extend Your love to those I see. In Jesus' name, Amen.

Day 335

God Fulfills His Word

A Truth to Live – It can seem at times like God has pushed "pause" or given a "delay" to the promises of His Word. In reality, in Jesus all the promises of God are now a "yes and amen". When His promises seem to be on hold I will ask God to reveal more of Himself to me so that I can know and understand His purposes more fully.

Scripture – "*The word of the LORD came to me: Son of man, what is this proverb you have in the land of Israel: 'The days go by and every vision comes to nothing'? Say to them, 'This is what the Sovereign LORD says: I am going to put an end to this proverb, and they will no longer quote it in Israel.' Say to them, 'The days are near when every vision will be fulfilled. For there will be no more false visions or flattering divinations among the people of Israel. But I the LORD will speak what I will, and it shall be fulfilled without delay. For in your days, you rebellious house, I will fulfill whatever I say, declares the Sovereign LORD'.*" Ezekiel 12:21-25

Prayer – Eternal God, I ask that You would align my thoughts, my will and my life to the power of Your Word. Help me to see the fulfillment of Your promises in my life! In Jesus' name, Amen.

Day 336

God's Love Puts Others First

A Truth to Live – I live in a "me first" generation where people focus their time and energy on self-benefiting plans and dreams. But God's ways are different. He has created me to love others, to think the best of them, to care for others and to bless those in need. When I follow His ways I always experience the power of His presence.

Scripture – "*The word of the LORD came to me: 'Son of man, prophesy against the shepherds of Israel; prophesy and say to them: This is what the Sovereign LORD says: Woe to the shepherds of Israel who only take care of themselves! Should not shepherds take care of the flock...You have not strengthened the weak or healed the sick or bound up the injured. You have not brought back the strays or searched for the lost. You have ruled them harshly and brutally. So they were scattered because there was no shepherd, and when they were scattered they became food for all the wild animals. My sheep wandered over all the mountains and on every high hill. They were scattered over the whole earth, and no one searched or looked for the'.*" Ezekiel 34:1-6

Prayer – Heavenly Father, How grateful I am today that Your love extends to me. Teach me to look after the needs of others just as You love and care for me. In Jesus' name, Amen.

Day 337

God Can Create a New Heart

A Truth to Live – God has the power to make all things new. He can restore areas of my heart that have been wounded by the words of others; mend relationships and bring hope to circumstances that look like they are beyond repair. He is good, He is God and He is ever powerful to share His life-giving love with others.

Scripture – "*I will give you a new heart and put a new spirit in you; I will remove from you your heart of stone and give you a heart of flesh.*" Ezekiel 36:26

Prayer – Gracious and Loving God, how I thank You for Your eternal love and Your commitment to create in me a clean and pure heart. Help me today to exchange my brokenness and weariness for the strength that comes from Your forgiving and cleansing love. In Jesus' name, Amen.

Day 338

God is the Great Rescuer

A Truth to Live – Placing my life in the hands of God is the best decision I will ever make. Since He created me and the world around me, He knows what is best and has the power to help me walk through the trials of life with hope, peace and the power of His love. Even if I feel that I have walked too far in the wrong direction to receive His free gift of forgiveness and love, God is still there waiting to rescue me back to Himself.

Scripture – "*I issue a decree that in every part of my kingdom people must fear and reverence the God of Daniel…For he is the living God and he endures forever; his kingdom will not be destroyed, his dominion will never end. He rescues and he saves; he performs signs and wonders in the heavens and on the earth. He has rescued Daniel from the power of the lions.*" Daniel 6:26-27

Prayer – Heavenly Father, thank You for helping me walk through the trials of life with hope, peace and power You provide, and that even when I take a wrong turn, You rescue me and bring me back to Your love. I am grateful for Your lovingkindness and forgiveness. In Jesus' name. Amen.

Day 339

God's Ways are the Best

A Truth to Live – Every decision I make has consequences that impact me and those around me. I can make the best choices when I am guided by the truth and power of God's Word. He knows how to navigate through life's twists and turns, and He is able to protect me from evil. Choosing His ways is always the best decision.

Scripture – "*But you must return to your God; maintain love and justice, and wait for your God always.*" Hosea 12:6

Prayer – Gracious and Eternal God, thank You for knowing which direction I should go, what words I should speak and how I should treat others. I am grateful that I can turn to You and find the answers to my needs today, hope and purpose for my tomorrows. You are great and so gracious and loving to share Your mercy with me. Thank You, in Jesus' name, Amen.

Day 340

God's Ways are Right

A Truth to Live – God has never made a mistake. He always knows what is right, does what is right and makes it possible for me to live right! He is powerful and personal, mighty and merciful and His greatest desire is to be able to share His love with me.

God's ways are found in His Word. They can heal my heart and shape my mind to make wise choices.

Scripture – "*The ways of the LORD are right; the righteous walk in them, but the rebellious stumble in them.*" Hosea 14:9b

Prayer – Eternal God, how I thank You today that Your ways are righteous and true. Help me to depend on Your wisdom today and not on the counsel of those who do not have my best interests in mind. I will praise You with all my being and be satisfied with Your direction. In Jesus' name, Amen.

Day 341

God's Directions Are Good

Truth – Ever been lost? The best way to find both where I am and where I want to be is to use an accurate map. Like many people, however, sometimes I rely on my own instincts to get me out of trouble. The next time I am faced with uncertainty or feel lost, I will choose God's ways and the truth of His Word. He is never wrong.

Scripture – "*The word of the LORD came to Jonah son of Amittai: 'Go to the great city of Nineveh and preach against it, because its wickedness has come up before me.' But Jonah ran away from the LORD and headed for Tarshish.*" Jonah 1:1-3a

Prayer – Heavenly Father, today I choose to listen to the strength of Your Word and direction of Your voice. Help me to not turn my attention to the opinions of others or even to depend on my own instincts. I know that You will be honored and I will be set on the right course when I follow You. In Jesus' name, Amen.

Day 342

God Loves Right and Hates Wrong

A Truth to Live – Every day my mind is filled with the opinions of others. I read about them in the newspaper, listen to them on the radio, watch them on TV or hear them from family and friends. But, there is One whose voice is real and true and whose word will never fail. When I listen to God, He will always lead me the right way.

Scripture – "*The LORD your God is with you, he is mighty to save. He will take great delight in you, he will quiet you with his love, he will rejoice over you with singing.*" Zephaniah 3:17

Prayer – Gracious and Loving Father, I am thankful for You! How awesome it is that my heart can be filled with Your Spirit and my mind filled with Your wisdom. I praise You today for Your loving-kindness and mercy that You have extended to me. In Jesus' name, Amen.

Day 343

Jesus is My Savior

A Truth to Live – I found it! The search is over right now. Knowing that left alone I couldn't find my way to a life of blessing and eternity with Him, God made a way for me to be united with Him! He sent His only Son, Jesus to be my Savior.

Scripture – "*She will give birth to a son, and you are to give him the name Jesus, because he will save his people from their sins.*" Matthew 1:21

Prayer – Heavenly Father, I am grateful today that the search is over. I no longer need to pursue other avenues of knowledge or religion to find peace in my heart! You have given me eternal life and blessings today through the life of Your Son, Jesus. I surrender anew to Him and receive Him as my Savior. In Jesus' name, Amen

Day 344

God Gives the Power to do Right

A Truth to Live – The standards of the world change with the seasons and are amended by new leaders, icons and the morals around me. But God's standard never changes. He expects righteous behavior, pure thoughts and a heart that is motivated toward Him. The only way for me to find salvation is through the grace offered to us by God's own Son.

Scripture – "*You have heard that it was said to the people long ago, 'Do not murder, and anyone who murders will be subject to judgment.' But I tell you that anyone who is angry with his brother will be subject to judgment. Again, anyone who says to his brother, 'Raca,' is answerable to the Sanhedrin. But anyone who says, 'You fool!' will be in danger of the fire of hell.*" Matthew 5:21-22

Prayer – Loving and Merciful God, I admit today that my heart is not inclined toward good and that my intentions are often misdirected. I ask that You rescue me from my own shortcomings and, by Your mighty hand, make a way for me to be saved. In Jesus' name, Amen.

Day 345

God Hears When I Pray

A Truth to Live – Every prayer offered to God matters. They don't bounce off the walls or fade away unnoticed. God hears and answers every prayer offered in faith and responds to those who believe in Him and in the saving power of His Son, Jesus Christ.

Scripture – "*If you believe, you will receive whatever you ask for in prayer.*" Matthew 21:22

Prayer – Heavenly Father, how I praise You today for being alive and caring for my needs. Thank You for listening to me and granting me the opportunity to believe and follow You. I believe in You and will expect Your good and righteous hand to direct my day. In Jesus' name, Amen.

Day 346

Jesus Made the Way

A Truth to Live – I was designed by God to be led by Him. But, I am surrounded by people who influence and shape my opinions and who offer direction for my life. God, however, made it very clear in His Word; there is just one way to find peace with Him, blessing on earth and eternal life – Jesus' sacrifice on the cross made it possible to have new life in God.

Scripture – "*While they were eating, Jesus took bread, gave thanks and broke it, and gave it to his disciples, saying, 'Take and eat; this is my body.' Then he took the cup, gave thanks and offered it to them, saying, 'Drink from it, all of you. This is my blood of the covenant, which is poured out for many for the forgiveness of sins'.*" Matthew 26:26-28

Prayer – Gracious Father, I come humbly to You today, knowing that You alone have the answers for my life. You alone can set me free from the bondage that holds me down and the darkness that deadens my heart. Thank You for the gift of life that comes through Your Son Jesus. His sacrifice on the cross has paved the way for my life in You. I receive Him as my Savior today and accept His Word as true. In Jesus' name, Amen.

Day 347

God Has Made an Invitation For Me

A Truth to Live – God has a plan for my life. It is good, filled with hope and promise, and it lasts forever. Even better, it is not complicated. While most of the self-help teachings and other religions of the world are filled with things to do, to remember and a list of rules to abide by, God's plan is so simple it is child-like. If I receive His Son as my Savior He will make me brand new!

Scripture – "*Let the little children come to me, and do not hinder them, for the kingdom of God belongs to such as these. I tell you the truth, anyone who will not receive the kingdom of God like a little child will never enter it.*" Mark 10:14b-15

Prayer – Eternal God, You are the life-giver. You know me and see all of my shortcomings yet, You still choose to love me and to forgive me. Thank You. Help me today to come in simple child-like faith and acknowledge You as my God. In Jesus' name, Amen.

Day 348

God Alone Has the Power to Cleanse and Empower

A Truth to Live – Each year thousands of new books are published offering new twists on the age old theme of self-help and work ethic. While it is true that practicing these principles can improve my life here on earth, they cannot prepare me for an eternity with God. Only God's Son, Jesus, has the power to cleanse and purify me to live with God forever.

Scripture – "*John answered them all, "I baptize you with water. But one more powerful than I will come, the thongs of whose sandals I am not worthy to untie. He will baptize you with the Holy Spirit and with fire.*" Luke 3:16

Prayer – Heavenly Father, thank You for the gift of eternal life. While others promise hope that doesn't seem to last, You have granted me the forgiveness of sin and replaced my broken heart with the power of Your Spirit. Help me today to walk in the cleansing power that comes from being baptized in You. In Jesus' name, Amen.

Day *349*

God Answers Prayer

A Truth to Live – There are some religions whose god is not alive and cannot hear or answer the cries of its followers. But the One True God is different. He can hear and His ears are turned toward me! He simply asks me to approach Him with my needs and desires so that He is put in a position to be my Provider, Guide and Sustainer.

Scripture – "*So I say to you: Ask and it will be given to you; seek and you will find; knock and the door will be opened to you. For everyone who asks receives; he who seeks finds; and to him who knocks, the door will be opened.*" Luke 11:9-10

Prayer – Gracious Father, thank You for listening to my prayers. All of them. To think that You are all powerful and yet take the time to dwell with me brings joy to my soul! Help me to remember to always ask You first and to seek Your ways. In Jesus' name, Amen.

Day 350

God Gives Eternal Life

A Truth to Live – Here is the best news ever. God loves me so much that, even though He knows me and has a record of what I have done, He wants to forgive me of all my sins. It is the absolutely best deal of all time. I can exchange all of my broken parts for His perfect love.

Scripture – *"For God so loved the world that he gave his one and only Son, that whoever believes in him shall not perish but have eternal life."* John 3:16

Prayer – God today I turn my thoughts toward You. I thank You for loving me so much that You sent Your only Son to die on the cross for my sins. I choose to believe in Him and receive eternal life with You. In Jesus' name, Amen.

Day 351

God's Way is Right

A Truth to Live – Life is full of authors, speakers and friends offering suggestions to help me find the right way to live my life well and to end it strong. Most suggest a good bit of self-discipline, hard work and kindness toward others. But in reality there is only one way to live that is completely satisfying, thoroughly peaceful and eternally good. It's God's way.

Scripture – *"Jesus answered, 'I am the way and the truth and the life. No one comes to the Father except through me'."* John 14:6

Prayer – Gracious Father, thank You for the power of Your Word. Rather than keep the keys to eternal life a secret You have shared them openly, even sending Your Son to show me the way. Help me today to make the right choice and to choose You. In Jesus' name, Amen.

Day 352

God Provides the Road Map to Life

A Truth to Live – There is absolutely no need to be lost, disoriented or confused about the important decisions in life. Why? Because God has provided the answers for me in His Word. The next step in my journey is to turn around and begin walking toward God. The Bible calls this repentance, and it is the most freeing, life-giving act I can ever choose.

Scripture – "*Peter replied, "Repent and be baptized, every one of you, in the name of Jesus Christ for the forgiveness of your sins. And you will receive the gift of the Holy Spirit.*" Acts 2:38

Prayer – Heavenly Father, today I choose to walk the path that You have given me. I admit that it is easy for me to stray, and so I ask that You help me to keep my eyes focused on You. I know that when I am immersed in thoughts of You and Your love for me I will walk the road of blessing that You have chosen for me. In Jesus' name, Amen.

Day 353

God's Love is Unstoppable

A Truth to Live – Throughout history evil empires, tyrants and dictators have caused pain, heartache, suffering and even death to those whose hearts are loyal to Jesus Christ. But the name of Jesus is more powerful than the darkest thought or the most evil act. His love can never be quenched.

Scripture – "*And Saul was there, giving approval to his death. On that day a great persecution broke out against the church at Jerusalem, and all except the apostles were scattered throughout Judea and Samaria. Godly men buried Stephen and mourned deeply for him. But Saul began to destroy the church. ... he dragged off men and women and put them in prison. Those who had been scattered preached the word wherever they went. Philip went down to a city in Samaria and proclaimed the Christ there. When the crowds heard Philip and saw the miraculous signs he did, they all paid close attention to what he said. With shrieks, evil spirits came out of many, and many paralytics and cripples were healed. So there was great joy in that city.*" Acts 8:1-8

Prayer – Almighty God, when my day is dark and my life seems isolated from hope I have confidence in You. Help me to face the brightest of days and discouraging moments knowing that You are King and Savior. I serve You alone. In Jesus' name, Amen.

Day 354

God Loves Cheerful Givers

A Truth to Live – Ever been in a one-sided relationship? The kind where someone asks things of you, but never returns the favor, refuels or revives you when you are weary? God-filled people are different. They love to give and they keep giving, because God continually fills them to overflowing.

Scripture – "*It is more blessed to give than to receive.*" Acts 20:35b

Prayer – Mighty and Ever-Generous Father, how grateful I am today that You are a giving God. You offered me love and forgiveness, redemption and wholeness and brokenness when I had nothing to offer You. Beginning today, help me to become a generous, giving person. Fill me to overflowing with Your hope and love so that I can bring joy to others. In Jesus' name, Amen.

Day 355

God is Our Redeemer

A Truth to Live – I admit that at some time I have been selfish with my actions, hurtful with my words and have not honored God with my responses. The simple word for these actions is sin. I don't deserve to stand before a perfect, loving and gracious God. I need a rescue.

Scripture – "*...for all have sinned and fall short of the glory of God, and are justified freely by his grace through the redemption that came by Christ Jesus.*" Romans 3:23-24

Prayer – Heavenly Father, You are filled with love and mercy, and I am overcome with guilt and shame. When I take a look at who I really am it is clear that I need a Savior and that You alone are the One who can rescue me from my own sin. Please forgive me of my wrongdoing, and come into my heart to rule, to reign and to guide me in the way of everlasting life. In Jesus' name, Amen.

Day 356

God Blesses Unity

A Truth to Live – My own human nature feeds my sense of insecurity and causes me to stand strongly for my ideals, even when it causes hurt among others. God never asks me to compromise with evil intentions, but He also wants me to work for peace and unity.

Scripture – "*I appeal to you, brothers, in the name of our Lord Jesus Christ, that all of you agree with one another so that there may be no divisions among you and that you may be perfectly united in mind and thought.*" 1 Corinthians 1:10

Prayer – Heavenly Father, I know that Your eyes look throughout the earth for those whose hearts are pure and actions are righteous. Help me to live in a way that honors You and blesses others. I know that where there is unity You will bring a blessing. In Jesus' name, Amen.

Day 357

God is Truth

A Truth to Live – God is Truth. He can be counted on for an accurate understanding of the past, a good read on the present and the right perspective for the future. As the Creator, Sustainer and Finisher of the earth, there is nothing that can take Him by surprise or cause Him to lie. He is truth and following Him will lead me and guide me to His goodness and blessing.

Scripture – "*I hope you will put up with a little of my foolishness; but you are already doing that. I am jealous for you with a godly jealousy. I promised you to one husband, to Christ, so that I might present you as a pure virgin to him. But I am afraid that just as Eve was deceived by the serpent's cunning, your minds may somehow be led astray from your sincere and pure devotion to Christ. For if someone comes to you and preaches a Jesus other than the Jesus we preached, or if you receive a different spirit from the one you received, or a different gospel from the one you accepted, you put up with it easily enough.*" 2 Corinthians 11:1-4

Prayer – Gracious Father, today I ask that You would lead my heart and my mind to Your truth. Keep me from straying in the wrong direction and guide me to everlasting life. In Jesus' name, Amen.

Day 358

God is Here

A Truth to Live – As the Creator of all things God is actively involved in both the big events and in the everyday activities of my life. He is the sustainer of the universe and the One who holds my life together. Even better, He is not distant or too pre-occupied with the crisis of the day to hear my prayer. He is God, He is good and He is a rewarder of those who diligently seek Him.

Scripture – "*There is one body and one Spirit - just as you were called to one hope when you were called - one Lord, one faith, one baptism; one God and Father of all, who is over all and through all and in all.*" Ephesians 4:4-6

Prayer – Eternal and All Powerful God, thank You for being in charge of my life. I admit that I am not capable of managing all the details, surprises and challenges that come across my path. Help me to know today that You are in charge, filled with goodness and blessing and that You have called me to You. In Jesus' name, Amen.

Day 359

God's Word is Good

A Truth to Live – Sometimes circumstances are troubling and I need insight and wisdom for the day. There is a place to turn that is guaranteed to give me the truth and provide a good, clear and concise journey to wisdom. It is God's Word.

Scripture – "*All Scripture is God-breathed and is useful for teaching, rebuking, correcting and training in righteousness, so that the man of God may be thoroughly equipped for every good work.*" 2 Timothy 3:16-17

Prayer – Heavenly Father, I am grateful today for the dependability of Your Word. It is always true, always good, and You breathed it into existence. More than just a good book it is life-giving and guides my day. Help me today to apply the richness of Your Word to my life. In Jesus' name, Amen.

Day 360

God Looks at the Big Picture

A Truth to Live – Many people separate their religion from their daily life. But, God doesn't separate what I believe from what I do. To Him, they are inseparable. In fact, He measures who I am by what I do and say. The best way forward in life is to read God's Word, believe what it says and do it!

Scripture – "*But someone will say, 'You have faith; I have deeds.' Show me your faith without deeds, and I will show you my faith by what I do.*" James 2:18

Prayer – Heavenly Father, help me to follow You today. I know that You have good things in store for me when I follow You. As I read Your Word and work to apply it in my life today, I ask that You give me strength to obey You. In Jesus' name, Amen.

Day 361

God Wants Me

A Truth to Live – God is not sitting in a distant throne room that is unapproachable and unreachable. He is here, alive and ready to meet me. He is patient, kind and desires that no one should perish. God wants to fulfill His promises on the earth through me.

Scripture – "*The Lord is not slow in keeping his promise, as some understand slowness. He is patient with you, not wanting anyone to perish, but everyone to come to repentance.*" 2 Peter 3:9

Prayer – Heavenly Father, thank You for being patient with me, for showing Your love and providing to me the richness of Your Word. Help me to reconcile my own heart with Your deep love and then to share Your goodness with others. In Jesus' name, Amen.

Day 362

God Wants the Best For Me

A Truth to Live – God is good and He is for me. Contrary to what I may have heard from others in school, at work or on TV God is not rude, unkind or merciless. In fact, His love for me is everlasting, and He orchestrated the very best plans for my present and my future. He wants nothing more than for me to walk with Him.

Scripture – "*But you, dear friends, build yourselves up in your most holy faith and pray in the Holy Spirit.*" Jude 1:20

Prayer – Eternal and Loving God, how I thank You today for knowing and planning out what is best for me. You know my skills, talents, weaknesses, and wounds, and You have planned out for me a purpose that is filled with joy and fulfillment. Teach me today, through the power of Your Word, to build myself up through the meditation of Your Word. In Jesus' name, Amen.

Day 363

God Can Make Me Brand New

A Truth to Live – I have made decisions in the past that I regret; said things that I wish I could take back; or done things that I wish could be erased from my life's record. The amazing truth of God's Word is that it reveals a Creator God who knows me inside and out. He knows all of my shortcomings, mistakes, and problems and chooses to make a way for me to find forgiveness, cleansing and healing. He is for my good.

Scripture – *"Behold I make all things new."*
Revelation 21:5

Prayer – God, today my prayer is simple. Take my life and cleanse it, make it brand new and restore hope in me through the power of Your Son Jesus Christ my Savior. In Jesus' name, Amen.

Day 364

God is the Victor

A Truth to Live – From the beginning of time until its end there has been one consistent drama unfolding on the earth. The key character is God, and it is His story. We know that He is merciful, kind, loving and filled with abundant goodness for all who choose to follow Him. God has been, is and will be victorious over every counterfeit power and the strongest forces of evil. He is Victory.

Scripture – "*The grace of the Lord Jesus be with God's people. Amen.*"

Prayer – Heavenly Father, thank You for the gift of Your Son, Jesus Christ in whom I have victory yesterday, today and forever. Help me walk away from the lure of evil and the distractions of the culture and instead cling to You, to live and abide by Your truth and to start and end each day in Your presence. In Jesus' name, Amen.

Day 365

God Loves Me

A Truth to Live – There is One whose love for me has never wavered and whose commitment to me is eternal. He is the One True God, and He is filled with forgiveness for every mistake and wrongdoing I have ever done. God is love and He loves me. No matter where I have been, what I have done or where I am headed God loves me.

Scripture – "*For God so loved the world that he gave his one and only Son, that whoever believes in him shall not perish but have eternal life.*" John 3:16

Prayer – Heavenly Father, today I make the commitment to follow You with my whole heart, mind, soul and strength. I believe in Your Son, Jesus and trust Him to be my Savior – both for today, tomorrow and for eternity. In Jesus' name, Amen.

27974308R00210

Made in the USA
Charleston, SC
28 March 2014